Troubled Waters
New Policies for Managing Water In the American West

Mohamed T. El-Ashry and
Diana C. Gibbons

WORLD RESOURCES INSTITUTE
A Center for Policy Research

Study 6
October 1986

I am not an advocate for frequent changes in laws and constitutions. But laws and institutions must go hand in hand with the progress of the human mind. As that becomes more developed, more enlightened, as new discoveries are made, new truths discovered and manners and opinions change, with the change of circumstances, institutions must advance also to keep pace with the times.

Thomas Jefferson
(From a letter to
Samuel Kercheval,
July 12, 1816)

Acknowledgments

This publication is the first product of WRI's Arid Lands Project. The project owes much to those who helped WRI in its early planning and to those who worked with us in later stages. We thank, in particular, the distinguished members of the advisory panel and the authors of the case studies, whose names and affiliations are listed in separate appendices at the conclusion of this study. In addition, we are indebted to Charles Meyers of Gibson, Dunn, and Crutcher in Denver, Colorado; Robert Hagan of the University of California at Davis; John Leshy of Arizona State University; Zach Willey of the Environmental Defense Fund in Berkeley, California; and Robert Repetto at WRI, all of whom reviewed a draft of this study and provided valuable comments and suggestions. Many of their suggestions were adopted, but the study remains the responsibility of the authors.

We also thank Kathleen Courrier, WRI's Publications Director, for editing and sharpening the manuscript; Hyacinth Billings for her efforts in producing the paper; Allyn Massey for designing the cover and drafting the figures; and Cynthia Veney, our project secretary. Finally, our sincere thanks to Gus Speth and Jessica Mathews, who provided much appreciated direction and support.

M.E.
D.G.

Foreword

Recently, two significant events took place in the long and colorful history of water issues in the American West. The governors of the western states issued a policy statement calling for sharply enhanced efficiency in water use, and the U.S. House of Representatives voted to prevent the Department of the Interior from completing a legal settlement with Westlands Water District that would cost taxpayers millions of dollars in the form of irrigation subsidies. Not only is the settlement a waste of scarce federal funds, but the water will irrigate large acreage of surplus crops for which there are no markets, and the runoff from the fields will add to the protracted pollution problems in the San Joaquin Valley. These events are indeed welcome news; they add to the impression that an important transition is underway in the traditional pork barrel politics of western water. But a lot more needs to be done if western states are to deal effectively with the increasing demands on their limited water resources while preserving the special environmental characteristics of the region that lead many people there in the first place.

Water is one of the West's most valuable assets. Of all the natural resources needed for economic growth, water has been the linchpin for successful development of arid and semi-arid western lands. As far back as 1902, federal programs establishing irrigated agriculture in the desert relied on massive water projects to harness and move water when and where it was needed. Now, thirsty cities and industries are rapidly expanding and vying for limited water supplies. At the same time, the traditional approach of large "structural measures" is increasingly challenged by fiscal realities and environmental constraints. The demands placed on oversubscribed water sources have resulted in water quality degradation, groundwater mining, and depletion of instream flows. Competition over western water is increasing among different economic sectors, among neighboring river basins, and between those who would develop water resources further and those who would protect other natural resources lost by that development. And federal funds are growing scarce.

Although impressive innovations have been made by some states on key issues, western water laws and institutions designed for an earlier era have not in general adapted to the new demands and stresses on water resources. In *Troubled Waters*, Mohamed El-Ashry and Diana Gibbons describe these laws and institutions, explore the nature of water demand in the agricultural and municipal sectors, and outline policies for maximizing the efficiency of water use and minimizing the conflicts inherent in policy change. They show how the West can move away from its historical reliance on expensive supply-side projects and subsidized water and toward better management and reallocation of existing supplies within water markets. And the prospects for environmental quality are enhanced in the process.

The American West is not unique in its water problems. About one third of the earth's surface is arid or semi-arid. In China, the Indian sub-continent, and the Middle East, all of which have been settled for a very long time, some lands are now being taken out of production because of irrigation-induced salinity. In the effort ''to make the desert bloom,'' water resources in many countries are being over-exploited, and some groundwater aquifers have been depleted. Numerous countries are also experiencing conflicts over the reallocation of limited supplies from agriculture to urban uses. Many of the recommendations included in *Troubled Waters*, when adapted to prevailing social, cultural, and economic conditions, could contribute to increasing the productivity of water and land resources in other regions.

This policy study grew out of a larger investigation by the World Resources Institute into current problems of land and water management in the drier regions of North America. Other aspects of this project deal with soil conservation policies in Canada and land and water management issues in northern Mexico.

An important event in this project occurred earlier this year. As part of its investigation, WRI commissioned six case studies that examine traditional agricultural and urban water use patterns and practices and outline emerging conflicts and possible policy actions. *(See Appendix A.)* On February 20 and 21, 1986, WRI convened a workshop in Tucson, Arizona to discuss the findings of the case studies. The 53 workshop participants included leading urban water utility managers, irrigation district managers, state and federal officials, environmentalists, economists, political scientists, and engineers, mostly from the western states. *(See Appendix B.)* While *Troubled Waters* is not strictly the outcome of this workshop, it did benefit greatly from the discussions and views presented there. The workshop was made possible through the generous financial support of the Joyce Foundation, for which we express our deep appreciation.

James Gustave Speth
President
World Resources Institute

Contents

I. Introduction

As a whole, the United States is a water-rich nation. The renewable water supply in the 48 conterminous states equals about 1,400 billion gallons a day—more than fourteen times the nation's daily water consumption.[1] Yet, despite this abundance, conflicts over water development and use are on the rise. Water supplies now appear inadequate in volume or quality to meet growing demands in many regions.

One facet of the nation's water crisis is masked by national averages: U.S. water riches are unevenly distributed among different geographic regions. In the arid and semi-arid regions of the West, water consumption averages 44 percent of renewable water supply and can be higher in dry years. This figure stands in contrast to an average of less than 4 percent everywhere else in the country.[2] Today, the arid western states face a host of water conflicts that, while typical of water conflicts occurring throughout the country, are in sharper focus because of the region's aridity. These western states illustrate the problems that rapid population and economic growth can cause where ecosystems are fragile and water resources limited.

The western sunbelt is one of the fastest-growing parts of the country owing to high indigenous growth rates, migration from other regions of the country, and legal and illegal immigration from countries to the south. Population growth in Arizona, for example, averaged 4.4 percent per year during the 1970s, with Tucson alone growing by over 50 percent during the decade.[3] Traditionally, most western water has fed irrigated agriculture, which

1

continues to be the dominant water user in every western state. But as cities expand and state economies diversify, attendant water demands for municipal, commercial, and industrial uses multiply. Particularly in the Colorado River Basin and in southern California, water supplies are sharply limited in relation to growing water demands that already require groundwater mining and importation from adjoining basins. And at the same time as offstream water demands have grown, the rise in public awareness of environmental quality has intensified competition for the remaining instream flows in rivers and lakes.

In the past, increased water demand was satisfied by developing new water sources. But environmental, engineering, and financial constraints make traditional supply-side responses less tenable than they once were. The local costs of transbasin diversions have gone up because the most efficient sites are already developed and the federal government is less willing to pick up the tab. The environmental opposition to large water projects has become more organized and more vocal, resorting to court battles alongside those groups protecting the interests of would-be water-exporting basins. Such competition between geographic regions with disparate water endowments has characterized the history of western water development and is intensifying as available supplies are over-taxed. It is abundantly clear that not all who want cheap, plentiful, and high quality water will get it.

It is abundantly clear that not all who want cheap, plentiful, and high quality water will get it.

While the prospects for meeting projected water demand solely through new supply projects and importation look slim, options for reducing demand growth, increasing efficiency of use, and reallocating existing supplies appear promising. Physical scarcity of water in the West has been compounded by economic scarcity—the lack of enough water to meet all the demands that arise when water is a free good. Water enough to meet society's needs is available, but incentives for its wise or conservative use are few, while impediments to achieving maximum benefits from the ofttimes minimal supplies are many. The efficient and equitable allocation of water among competing demands thus looms as a major policy challenge for the future.

Because irrigated agriculture has long been the major consumer of western water, many observers

> One unfortunate legacy of rules developed when water supplies were vast in relation to the needs of an economically nascent region is an apportionment system with built-in incentives that thwart flexibility in water use patterns and discourage water conservation.

see it as a logical source to tap for quenching cities' growing thirst. Yet, existing policies, laws, and institutions have not adapted to the very difficult problem of water reallocation under the new paradigm of economic scarcity. One unfortunate legacy of rules developed when water supplies were vast in relation to the needs of an economically nascent region is an apportionment system with built-in incentives that thwart flexibility in water use patterns and discourage water conservation. Water is free to those individuals who appropriate it for use, and prices charged to consumers by cities or other umbrella entities are quite low. Unlike most other commodities, water is not traded in a marketplace but allocated within a bureaucratic and legal system, a policy that may not best serve a rapidly growing and urbanizing West. Most of the institutions created when irrigated agriculture was the region's dominant economic and political force do not yet show the flexibility needed to reallocate fully-appropriated water supplies as the balance of power shifts from farm to city.

Existing policies do not adequately protect water quality either. Traditional management practices have led to land and water-quality degradation. The evidence, now common, includes soil erosion, land subsidence, soil salinization and waterlogging, high salinity levels in ground and surface waters, and toxic elements in surface and subsurface return flows. These negative consequences of some water uses are being borne by downstream water users and by society as a whole.

Given these myriad water problems of both quantity and quality, the challenge facing western states is to increase the productivity of water resources while equitably distributing the costs and benefits of water use. The level of current debate over water problems in the West merely underscores the tremendous opportunity at hand for improving water policy. The chance to raise the returns to water resources in the West, while enhancing environmental protection, should not be passed over.

Fortunately, policies and institutions in some places are slowly evolving to meet new water needs. But more change is needed. The purpose of this study is twofold: to explore the nature of the West's emerging water problems and to uncover solutions that are both politically feasible and economically viable. Fortunately, ample evidence indicates that effective and realistic policies do exist for improving efficiency and maximizing the benefits of water use, policies that can be implemented within the existing legal framework, including the doctrine of prior appropriation.

Within a particular economic sector, such as the municipal sector, water use could be much more efficient if conservation programs and marginal cost pricing strategies were employed. Household water consumption is responsive to water price, and peoples' habits do change in response to incentives. The cities of the arid West need to examine least-cost strategies for meeting and managing their burgeoning water demands and to take a critical look at their underlying attitudes about urban growth in a desert or semi-arid environment.

The agricultural sector will undoubtedly be a target for many new water-management policies in the West as well. Several states have recognized the necessity of removing barriers to water conservation, such as restrictions on the resale of salvaged or conserved water. And free market forces allowed to act through institutions such as water banks will go a long way toward alleviating supply inadequacies. With greater competition, some irrigation water supplies will be transferred to other uses as irrigation efficiencies rise, a move that may also help reduce salinity and other water quality problems. Clearly, removing impediments to the movement of water supplies among economic sectors is at the heart of policy reform.

Impediments to basin-wide efficiency also thrive under current interstate institutions. Communication and cooperation among various state and federal entities will be vital in shaping the Colorado River Basin's future, for example. That future could hold innovative interstate water markets that would increase the total benefits from the Colorado River and divide those benefits more equitably.

As part of any proposed policy, the government has a distinct role in correcting the traditional market failures, such as third party damages or environmental degradation. Instream flows also need protection, perhaps through state appropriation or regulation of minimum standards. For the most part, policies that enhance the productivity and mobility of water supplies and streamline water demands could help the states of the West sustain economic prosperity without

> For the most part, policies that enhance the productivity and mobility of water supplies and streamline water demands could help the states of the West sustain economic prosperity without undervaluing or destroying their natural resources, particularly the environmental amenities most westerners prize.

undervaluing or destroying their natural resources, particularly the environmental amenities most westerners prize.

II. The West in Profile

From the grasslands of west Texas to the deserts of Arizona, the southwest quadrant of the United States is the most arid part of the country. The Great Plains states, with their vast farmlands and grazing lands, are semi-arid and relatively flat. To the West, the Rocky Mountains and other ranges in Colorado and New Mexico rise out of the plains to form the massive peaks of the Continental Divide. These mountains shelter some well-watered valleys before giving way to arid basins and deserts in Nevada, Utah, and Southern California. The arid and semi-arid West is thus quite varied in terrain and local climate.

Of the 1.9 billion acres of land in the contiguous United States, almost half are in the arid and semi-arid region, which receives less than 20 inches of precipitation per year.[4] *(See Figure 1.)* Water supplies in the West are both limited and variable. Rainfall and snowfall are unevenly distributed across the states and areas within a state. For example, average rainfall in the mountainous area surrounding Flagstaff, Arizona measures over 20 inches per year. But in central and southern Arizona, where most of the people live and most of the agricultural areas are located, average rainfall ranges from only 7 inches (in Phoenix) to 11 inches per year (in Tucson).[5]

Almost more important than the quantity of rainfall for western water users is the natural variation in supplies from season to season, year to year, and even decade to decade. For example, Tucson gets most of its rainfall during summer thunderstorms between July and September. Much of this precipitation is lost through evaporation and transpiration, so surface runoff is

7

limited and unpredictable. Throughout the West, seasonal variation in streamflows is also governed by the springtime melt of the heavy snowpacks in the mountains, forming the headwaters of all western rivers. Even long-term streamflows show great variation. As Figure 2 illustrates, the historical annual flow of the Colorado River exhibits persistent wet and dry cycles measurable in decades.

Figure 1: Average Annual Precipitation

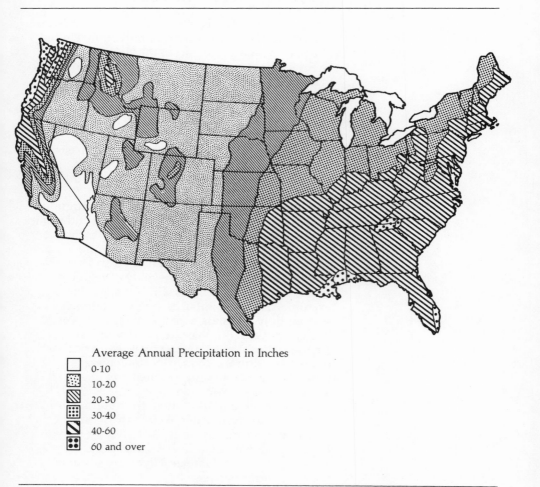

Average Annual Precipitation in Inches
- 0-10
- 10-20
- 20-30
- 30-40
- 40-60
- 60 and over

Source: Veronica I. Pye, Ruth Patrick, and John Quarles, *Groundwater Contamination in the United States* (Philadelphia: University of Pennsylvania Press, 1983) fig. 3-6

Figure 2: Annual Runoff of the Upper Colorado River

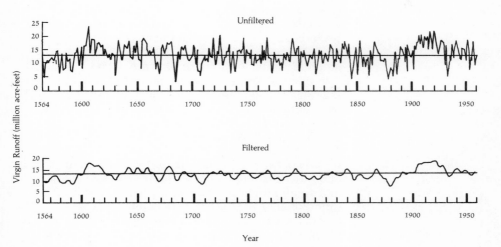

Tentative 400-year reconstruction of annual runoff at Lee Ferry, Arizona. This reconstruction is based on tree-ring chronologies within the Upper Colorado River Basin collected as part of the Lake Powell Research Project and on chronologies that were in the files of the Laboratory of Tree-Ring Research.

Source: Gordon C. Jacoby, Jr., ''An Overview of the Effect of Lake Powell on Colorado River Basin Water Supply and Environment,'' Lake Powell Research Project Bulletin No. 14 (Institute of Geophysics and Planetary Physics at the University of California at Los Angeles, November 1975) fig. 4

The other source of water in the West is groundwater—a generic term for various subterranean supplies. Some groundwater supplies are interconnected with surface flows while other supplies are held in place by impermeable rock layers. These less mobile supplies are often referred to as confined or artesian aquifers. In some cases, ages-old water that is recharged almost imperceptibly is referred to as fossil water. All of these types of groundwater supplies are found in the West. For example, the portion of the Ogallala aquifer that underlies much of the High Plains of Texas is ancient and is rapidly being depleted. Similar aquifers can be found in southern Arizona.

In many areas of the West, natural ecosystems are fragile. The rangelands of the plains suffer frequent and prolonged dry spells that, along with wind erosion, threaten everything but the tumbleweeds. Soil erosion poses a serious environmental threat to the cultivated plains. The deserts of the Southwest are home to the cactus and other plants that have adapted to the dry soil and air and that can withstand a temperature differential of 50° to 60 °F between the hot days and chilly nights. Overall, the lack of precipitation, the thin soils, and climatic extremes combine to create a harsh and unforgiving environment to which flora and fauna must adapt. Once the natural ecosystems and indigenous species are disrupted and replaced with irrigated agriculture, for example, they may take centuries to get re-established when farmlands are abandoned.

The early history of the American West was marked by tremendous in-migration beginning in the last half of the nineteenth century.[6] Two developments in the course of the settlement of the West necessitated a legal doctrine for water allocation that was adapted to the extremely arid conditions of much of the land—the discovery of gold and silver in the western mountains and the widespread use of irrigation in crop production. Most ore deposits were removed from watercourses; to work a claim, except by panning in streambeds, miners had to divert stream water in flumes and pipes. Thus, a body of informal water law grew up in the mining camps. As it happened, the procedures by which gold and silver claims were established and worked were easily transferred from ore to water. The first person to file a claim to mine was allowed priority over any later claimants. To remain the owner of a mining claim, one had to stake it, take possession of it, and "work" the claim productively.

The water law that grew up in the mining camps was termed the "prior appropriation doctrine." Later, this influential doctrine was adopted by irrigators, whose diversion needs in the arid climate were similar to the miners'. The "first in time, first in right" priority system gave security of supply in times of drought to those with early claims. The right to use water was exclusive, absolute, and established by the act of diversion.

As the West grew and states codified their legal systems, some of the basic tenets of the prior appropriation doctrine gradually eroded. In practice, it became clear that third-party damages were rampant. Since diversion rights were defined in terms of withdrawal quantities, and one user's return flows were another's source of supply, any change in point of diversion or type of use affected appropriators (third parties) downstream. Legislators attempted to correct these third-party effects and the incidence of inflated claims by adding restrictive clauses to the doctrine, such as beneficial and reasonable use requirements, land appurtenancy rules that tie water use to a particular parcel of land, and compensation to parties injured by transfers. Often, these clauses were adopted from riparian water law, with which judges imported from the East were familiar. Under the riparian doctrine, rights to use water are shared by those owning land alongside the stream.

While "beneficial use" became the basis for an appropriator's water right, efficiency criteria were not expressly defined. Instead, custom and tradition dictated the quantity of water considered reasonable. A water right could be lost if not put to beneficial use over a specified time—hence, the common admonition "use it or lose it."[7]

Which combination of water laws each state adopted often depended on how arid the land was. The Pacific coastal states with plentiful surface supplies adopted features of both prior appropriation and riparian doctrines, while the dry interior states use prior appropriation water law exclusively. Laws governing the allocation of groundwater supplies likewise vary by state and range from full prior appropriation to absolute ownership to correlative and beneficial use doctrines.

Each western state developed different institutions for implementing its legal doctrines. In New Mexico, a state engineer makes decisions on water transfers and changes in point of diversion or type of use. In Colorado, a system of water courts adjudicates conflicts over water rights. In most states, it is up to water right holders to prove that altering their use will not violate the rights of downstream users.

As the individual states of the West developed legal definitions and allocation rules for water rights within their borders, it became apparent that the major rivers also needed to be apportioned among the states. The Colorado River Compact, the agreements hammered out among the states in both the Upper and Lower Basins, congressional acts, and rulings by the U.S. Supreme Court together allocate the waters of the Colorado River to all the states through which they flow. If an Upper Basin state cannot use its share, that water continues downstream to the Lower Basin states, where it is further allocated to agricultural and urban interests through a priority system.

Significantly, the historic negotiations during 1922 for the Colorado River Compact took place near the end of a twenty-year wet cycle for the Colorado River. The amount of water available over the long term now appears to be considerably less than was assumed a half-century ago, so the balance of entitlements is somewhat skewed in favor of the Lower Basin states. While the Compact allocates 7.5 million acre-feet (maf) to both the Upper and Lower Basins, it obliges the Upper Basin to deliver 75 maf to the Lower Basin in any ten-year period. The data show the long-run average yearly flow of the Colorado River may be as low as 13.5 maf.[8]

Complicating the development of water law and allocation in the West were the economies of scale in water projects that came to light as agriculture grew. Farmers had to band together to afford such large-scale works as reservoirs for storing flows from one season to the next and conveyance networks for moving large quantities of water. State governments recognized the need for local organizations to oversee these works and allowed farmers to form quasi-governmental entities with the power to require membership of all beneficiaries. These "districts" retain substantial powers of property taxation and water-use regulation within their jurisdictions, as well as tax-exempt status, and to this day they are major power brokers in the development, allocation, and management of water supplies in the West.[9]

Although large projects in the West were initially privately funded and constructed, the federal government soon stepped in to hasten and encourage the economic growth and settlement of the West. The Reclamation Act of 1902 is recognized as the beginning of many decades of federal involvement in constructing and subsidizing water projects in the West. The U.S. Bureau of Reclamation was established to construct federally financed dams and other works and to contract water deliveries with the local beneficiaries (usually irrigation districts). The required reimbursement by the beneficiaries was based on their "ability to pay," a loosely calculated rate that ensures the solvency of farms as well as government's ultimate failure to collect full repayment. Bureau subsidies added later included long-term contracts at little or no interest with periods of suspended payments, extension of repayment periods, and below-cost electric power rates for water pumping. Eventually, even the 160-acre maximum farm size was abandoned. In California's Central Valley Project (CVP), only $50 million, or about 5 percent of the total $931 million spent on the project's irrigation facilities over the last 40 years, has been repaid to date. Since the current average water price is $6.15 per acre-foot, the subsidy amounts to more than 90 percent of the actual cost of $72.99 per acre-foot.[10]

As the presence of irrigated agriculture in the West was ensured by federal subsidies, other economic sectors grew rapidly, especially after World War I. Cities sprang up in the desert with a wide array of support industries as people moved and traveled to the sunbelt to enjoy the warm, dry climate, the blue skies, and the abundant scenic beauty. Many would argue that the American West is still a frontier—the landscape is sparsely populated, with only 17 people per square mile, on average, in New Mexico, Colorado, Utah, Nevada, and Arizona. (The average figure for the entire United States is 64 people per square mile.)[11] The low average population density, however, belies the number of people for whom the West is home. Today, almost 30 million people live there, and the biggest increases are recent, with the population up 27 percent in the 1960s and

Common perceptions notwithstanding, the West has become the most urban region of the country.

29 percent in the 1970s.[12] Today, the populace is concentrated in such large metropolitan centers as Denver, Phoenix, Salt Lake City, and Los Angeles. The percentage of the population living in metropolitan areas ranges from a high of 95 percent in California to a low of 42 percent in New Mexico and averages 76 percent throughout the region.[13] In fact, common perceptions notwithstanding, the West has become the most urban region of the country.[14]

By and large, water has to be brought to western cities, often from distant sources. Although most cities sprang up alongside rivers, their needs for water long ago outstripped the local surface supplies. Even small cities in the West depend increasingly on imported water. In spite of geographical and climatic limitations, these urban oases manage to thrive and grow, more with the help of technological prowess (in the form of water-import infrastructures) than by environmental adaption. Now, the region's economy is full and broad; the government's goal of promoting development has succeeded. Despite the arid climate and the ofttimes inhospitable environment, the desert has blossomed, the West has been tamed, and its impressive growth continues.

III. Irrigation and Agriculture

Although municipal and industrial water needs are growing, water use in the West continues to be dominated by irrigated agriculture. Everything from alfalfa to pecans can be grown in the desert if enough water is added to the soil. Even in the semi-arid lands where dryland farming is possible, yields are boosted and anxieties over uncertain precipitation are vanquished with the use of irrigation systems.

Consumptive use for irrigation is the largest single water use in the United States, often reaching 90 percent of total water consumption in western states.[15] *(See Table 1.)* Agricultural water use has the highest consumption-to-withdrawal ratio, which means that relatively more of the water diverted from streams or aquifers evaporates from the soil or transpires from crops instead of returning to the sources for reuse. This ratio averages about 60 percent, compared to 25 percent in municipal use and between 0 and 25 percent in industrial use.[16]

Nationally, irrigation is a significant factor in the success and size of the agricultural economy. Although irrigated farms make up only one seventh of all agricultural lands, they contribute more than one fourth of the total value of crop production.[17] Irrigated acreage increased from about 4 million in 1890 to nearly 60 million in 1977, and about 50 million of these acres are located in the 17 western states.[18] Although total irrigated acreage in the United States is still growing, the areas experiencing growth are in southeastern states and elsewhere.

The most important determinant of the total number of irrigated acres is undoubtedly the

> **Consumptive use for irrigation is the largest single water use in the United States, often reaching 90 percent of total water consumption in western states.**

Table 1. Irrigated Acreage and Water Use

State	Irrigated Land (Acres) 1982	Irrigated Land as a Percentage of Total Cropland 1982	Consumptive Water Use (Million Gallons/ Day) 1980	Percentage of Total Consumptive Use 1980
Arizona	1,153,478	74%	4,000	89%
California	8,460,508	75	23,000	92
Colorado	3,200,942	30	3,600	90
Nevada	829,761	96	1,500	88
New Mexico	807,206	36	1,700	89
Texas	5,575,553	14	8,000	80
Utah	1,082,328	56	2,400	83

Sources: Acreage and land use data are from U.S. Department of Commerce, Bureau of the Census, *Agricultural Census 1981*; Water use data are from U.S. Geological Survey, *National Water Summary 1983-Hydrologic Events and Issues*, Water Supply Paper No. 2,250 (Washington, D.C.: U.S. Government Printing Office, 1984).

overall crop price index. When national or international supply and demand cause the prices of food and fiber to fall, acreage decreases as well. Thus, unless crop prices rise substantially, water demand for agriculture in the West is not expected to grow. In fact, Bureau of Reclamation data show a sustained decline in irrigated acres in the West since 1979 (with the exception of 1982) and an increase since 1966 in land used for purposes other than crop production (e.g., residential, commercial, and industrial purposes).[19] In many areas, irrigated agriculture is threatened by the expansion of suburbs into the countryside. Urban encroachment is quite evident in metropolitan Phoenix and on the front range of Colorado, where a string of cities from Colorado Springs to Fort Collins has advanced into formerly agricultural and grazing lands.

The water for western irrigation comes from several sources and through several institutional arrangements. Farms that use surface water may own appropriative rights, but are more likely part of an irrigation district or a mutual water company that holds appropriative rights or contracts for water from federal or state projects. The farmer owns shares in the ditch company, which are entitlements to water or contracts for water from the irrigation district; in neither case does the farmer hold the water right except through the umbrella organization.

Much of the water supplied to irrigators originates in state or federal (Bureau of Reclamation) water projects subsidized by taxpayers, so it is very inexpensive to the farmer. When combined with "use it or lose it" provisions in state water law and restrictions on use and on size and timing of return flow, these subsidies are a disincentive to conserving surface water. As long as water is cheap, it will be used inefficiently. And if farmers cannot consider the opportunity cost of retaining water for irrigation, perhaps because resale or leasing is prohibited, they have no reason to ensure that the economic return to water used for growing crops approaches that in alternative uses.[20]

An exception to the norm of low water prices occurs when groundwater is used for irrigation. Farmers who rely on groundwater merely pump the water as needed, subject to state laws on pumping rates and well spacing. Since energy costs comprise the bulk of water-procurement costs for these farms, the rise in energy prices since 1974 has eroded profit margins and forced some farmers to conserve water. In many places, the conservation effect of higher energy prices is compounded by ever greater pumping depths caused by mining of the underlying aquifers. As the costs associated with pumping groundwater have become prohibitive in places, most notably in parts of Texas and central California, the productivity of water use has increased. More efficient pumps and irrigation systems have become economic to install and management practices have been adapted to the increased water scarcity. Rising water costs have also triggered shifts to higher-valued crops and to those crops that need less water to grow. When water costs make irrigated crop production less profitable, irrigated acreage finally reverts back to dryland farming, or it is abandoned. In the High Plains of Texas overlying the Ogallala aquifer and in other isolated areas of the West, this shift is already occurring.[21]

The economic value of irrigation water depends on a number of factors, including which crops are grown and how efficiently water is used. Low-valued crops—alfalfa and pasture, corn, sorghum, barley, wheat, and other small grains—account for about 74 percent of all irrigated acres in the West.

> **If farmers cannot consider the opportunity cost of retaining water for irrigation, perhaps because resale or leasing is prohibited, they have no reason to ensure that the economic return to water used for growing crops approaches that in alternative uses.**

In contrast, vegetable crops and fruit orchards have high average irrigation water values, but comprise only 9 percent of total acreage.[22] In the middle range are cotton, soybeans, and other crops, which claim extensive acreage. *(See Table 2.)* Notably, as the efficiency of water use goes up, the value of water for growing the crop rises. According to one analysis, the marginal value of water for growing cotton rose from $61 to $94 per acre-foot as efficiency increased from average (50–70 percent) to high levels (60–80 percent).[23]

Strictly, irrigation efficiency is a measure of how much of the water applied to a field is actually used by the plants. Water not used for crop evapotranspiration may evaporate (especially if applied by sprinkler systems in arid climates), seep into the earth, or drain from the land as surface return flow. Some portion of the water seepage moves down through the soil and subsoil to the groundwater table, though some

Table 2. Crop Water Values from Three Arizona Studies (dollars per acre-foot)

	water value[a]		
Crop	Willitt, Hathorn and Robertson (1975)	Kelso, Martin, and Mack (1974)	Martin and Snyder (1979)
Grain Sorghum	-1	3-28	23
Barley	5	27-35	32
Alfalfa	20	25-41	24
Wheat	18	30-32	40
Cotton	28-40	89-166	51-65
Vegetables	—	>117	>118

Source: Gayle S. Willitt, Scott Hathorn, Jr., and Charles E. Robertson, ''The Economic Value of Water Used to Irrigate Field Crops in Central and Southern Arizona, 1975,'' Department of Agricultural Economics Report #9 (Tucson, University of Arizona, September 1975); Maurice M. Kelso, William E. Martin, and Lawrence E. Mack, *Water Supplies and Economic Growth in an Arid Environment* (Tucson, University of Arizona press, 1974) pp. 122–126; William E. Martin and Gary B. Snyder, ''Valuation of Water and Forage from the Salt-Verde Basin of Arizona,'' Report to the U.S. Forest Service (September 1979).
[a]All values were converted to ''1980'' values by use of individual crop price indices. Dashes = not applicable.

percolating water can be lost to the system for years. System-wide efficiency is further reduced by the seepage and evaporation losses that are inevitable in conveying water from the source. Irrigation efficiency is affected by the type of technology employed and the capital investment in the land and physical structures. Canals and ditches lined with concrete or plastic increase water delivery efficiency by lessening seepage, irrigation scheduling and water-saving equipment (such as trickle irrigation systems) increase on-farm efficiency by lowering evaporative losses, and laser-leveling the land reduces runoff.

Under present irrigation practices, crops use only about half of the water applied.[24] And irrigation return flows, whether surface or subsurface, cause many water quality problems. Runoff from agricultural lands is often degraded by salts, sediments, pesticides, nutrients, or even such toxic trace elements as selenium.

The major water quality problem in the arid and semi-arid western states is salinity, which affects nearly every river basin. River waters become more saline from the headwaters to the mouths as seepage and return flows from irrigated lands empty into the rivers. For example, the salinity concentration in New Mexico's Pecos River increases from 760 to 2,020 milligrams per liter in just 30 miles. In Texas' Rio Grande River, salinity increases from 870 to 4,000 milligrams per liter in 75 miles.[25]

The salinity levels in several western rivers result partly from natural saline springs and erodible salt-containing rock formations. For example, saline springs near Glenwood Springs and Dotsero, Colorado, add more than 500,000 tons of salt to the Colorado River annually.[26] In fact, as much as half of the average salt load of the Colorado River may result from natural sources.[27]

In many areas, groundwater is severely polluted by deep percolation of irrigation water and seepage from irrigation-conveyance systems. The groundwater system can act as a conduit for saline wastewater to enter rivers. In Colorado's Grand Valley, for example, about 145,800 acre-feet of irrigation water enter the groundwater system every year, contributing about 500,000 to 700,000 tons of salt annually to the Colorado River.[28]

Salinity is not just a problem of instream water quality. Soil salinity poses a major threat to agriculture in the West and can worsen as saline

The major water quality problem in the arid and semi-arid western states is salinity.

19

water is used for irrigation or as waterlogging of poorly-drained lands occurs. The lack of drainage in many agricultural areas causes the water table to rise, subjecting the productive soil layer to severe salinization and reducing crop yields. By 1990, an estimated 2.2 million acres of land in the fertile San Joaquin Valley will have water tables at a depth of five feet or less, and 1.6 million acres will require expensive drainage schemes to stay in production.[29]

An estimated 10 million acres in the West (about 20 percent of all irrigated land) suffer from salt-caused yield reductions.[30] The Colorado River Basin (including the Imperial and Coachella Valleys of southern California that receive Colorado River water) has the greatest salinity problems. But it is followed closely by the Rio Grande Basin of New Mexico and Texas and the Central Valley of California, including the San Joaquin Valley.[31] *(See Figure 3.)*

Each year, salinity causes millions of dollars in damages to agriculture, as well as to industrial and municipal water users, and these costs are increasing. In agriculture, the costs are reduced productivity and restriction to salt-tolerant but less profitable crops. Crop yield losses begin when the salt concentration in irrigation water reaches 700 to 850 milligrams per liter, depending on soil conditions and crop type. (For drinking water, the upper limit recommended by the U.S. Environmental Protection Agency (EPA) is 500 milligrams per liter of total dissolved solids.)[32] Municipal, commercial, and industrial water users suffer the corrosive effects of salinity on plumbing, industrial boilers, and household appliances, and are faced with increases in water-treatment costs.

The total cost of salinization is considerable. In the Colorado River Basin, where detailed estimates of damage costs are available, the heavy salt load of 9–10 million tons annually is costing all users more than $113 million a year (in 1982 dollars), and that estimate is expected to more than double by 2010 if controls are not instituted.[33] In the San Joaquin Valley, crop yields have declined 10 percent with financial losses of $31.2 million annually since 1970 because of high saline water tables, and the losses are expected to mount to $321.3 million by 2000 if no action is taken.[34]

In all the affected rivers and river basins in the West, salinity problems have worsened progressively as water resources have been

In the Colorado River Basin, the heavy salt load of 9–10 million tons annually is costing all users more than $113 million a year.

Figure 3: Areas with Major Salinity Problems In The Western United States

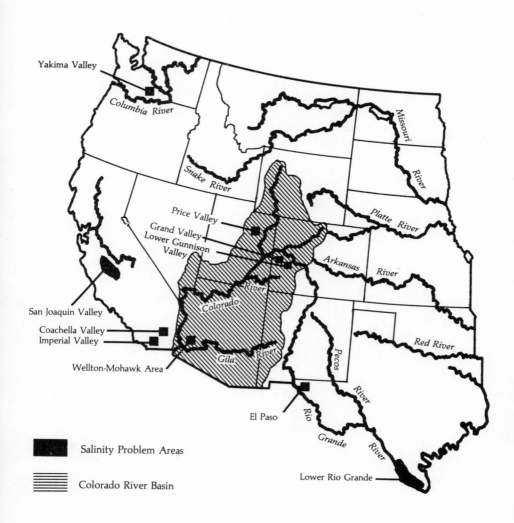

Yakima Valley

Columbia River

Snake River

Missouri River

Price Valley
Grand Valley
Lower Gunnison Valley

Platte River

Arkansas River

San Joaquin Valley

Coachella Valley
Imperial Valley

Colorado River

Wellton-Mohawk Area

Gila River

Red River

Pecos River

El Paso

Rio Grande River

Salinity Problem Areas

Colorado River Basin

Lower Rio Grande

Source: Mohamed T. El-Ashry, Jan van Schilfgaarde, and Susan Schiffman, "Salinity Pollution from Irrigated Agriculture," *Journal of Soil and Water Conservation,* vol. 40, no. 1 (January-February 1985) p. 49

developed. This trend will continue with future water development unless those water users contributing to the quality degradation face the damages and comprehensive, basin-wide water quality management schemes are instituted.

IV. Case Studies of Agricultural Water Demand

The Central Valley of California

The Central Valley has long been one of the premier agricultural areas of California, if not the nation.[35] The Valley is divided into three hydrographic basins with the bulk of rainfall (22 inches mean annual precipitation) and surface flow (largely from snowmelt in the neighboring mountains) originating in the northern Sacramento basin. The central San Joaquin basin receives about 13 inches of rainfall per year, while the Tulare Lake basin in the south averages only 6 inches per year on the valley floor. In their unimpaired state, the northern Central Valley rivers drained to the ocean through the Sacramento-San Joaquin Delta and the San Francisco Bay. But due to reservoir and aqueduct construction, the San Joaquin Basin now has reduced outflows and the Tulare Lake Basin is closed, with outflows occurring only in extremely wet years.

Water for irrigation is brought from the northern basin of the Central Valley to the central and southern basins in several canals. These large works were built under the auspices of either the state of California (the State Water Project, or SWP) or the United States Bureau of Reclamation (the Central Valley Project, or CVP). The SWP moves water from the Sacramento Basin south in the California Aqueduct along the west side of the San Joaquin Valley and delivers irrigation water to agricultural users in the San Joaquin and Tulare

Lake basins. Municipal and industrial deliveries are pumped over the Tahachapi Mountains into the Los Angeles Basin. Among other elements of the CVP system, the main canal, Friant Kern, moves water from the San Joaquin River south along the east side of the San Joaquin Valley into the Tulare Lake basin. *(See Figure 4)*.

Since surface flows for a substantial portion of agriculture in the Central Valley originate in these large projects, the irrigation districts that contract for supplies are powerful and important institutions. One interesting facet of the Central Valley is the price differential that exists between water originating in state and federal projects, with heavily subsidized water from the CVP less than half the cost of water from the SWP. For example, water in the Westlands Water District (CVP contractor) cost $16 per acre-foot in 1985, while water in nearby Lost Hills Water District (SWP contractor) cost $35 and SWP contractors further south along the aqueduct paid as much as $65 per acre-foot. This price differential creates a "two-tiered" surface water price system for agriculture in California, with corresponding tiers of water use efficiency.

The Central Valley's other source of irrigation water is groundwater, which accounts for 45 percent of the water supply. Groundwater supplies are recharged by a combination of precipitation, percolation, over-irrigation, and artificial recharge. Because of the interrelationship between surface and groundwater, conjunctive use is practiced to maximize water supplies and protect groundwater sources from rapid depletion. Nonetheless, yearly groundwater utilization in the Central Valley includes approximately 1.5 million acre-feet of overdraft. The central and southern basins of the Valley contain eight sub-basins designated as critically overdrawn.

Irrigated crop production in the Central Valley is currently facing problems of both water quantity and water quality. In some areas, groundwater mining might continue for many years without reaching the point of economic exhaustion of the aquifer. But some areas are already nearing that day, and eventually groundwater pumpage will have to be decreased.

The Central Valley's need for more water could be alleviated by increasing irrigation efficiency and improving the mobility of supplies. Transferring

Figure 4: Major Features of the State Water Project And The Central Valley Project

Source: Adapted from California Department of Water Resources, "California Water Plan: Projected Use and Available Water Supplies to 2010." Bulletin 160–83 (December 1983)

and exchanging supplies within an irrigation district is a fairly straightforward transaction. However, transfers and exchanges between districts and basins are harder to effect since the districts must approve all transactions and act as brokers. Furthermore, U.S. Bureau of Reclamation policies that allow transfers of federal water from one irrigator to another may preclude the transfer of at least some of the subsidies to non-agricultural uses. Yet, because the valley floor is criss-crossed with canals, many such transfers are physically feasible. Clearly, an increase in trading would increase the overall efficiency of water use in the Central Valley.

Plans to build additional segments of the State Water Project to increase reliable supplies have met with resistance. An improved through-delta facility might increase the security of supplies to farmers in drought years but represents a very expensive insurance policy. Incremental cost estimates for the facility are $68 per acre-foot, or an increase of $9 per acre-foot in the average cost of SWP water. The current climate for agricultural profits is not encouraging either. While the economic rents (that is, profits) to irrigators stemming from subsidized water costs will forestall a real decline in agriculture, the Central Valley has not been immune to the cost-price squeeze affecting the United States agricultural sector as a whole.

Another problem for Central Valley agriculture is water quality degradation from residuals, both salts and toxic elements, in irrigation return flows. On the valley floor, saline irrigation return flows pour into the streams and rivers, raising instream salinity levels. Inflows to the San Joaquin Basin from the Sierra Nevada Range show a salt concentration of 51 milligrams per liter (mg/l) at Millerton Lake. Fifty miles downstream, the maximum concentration reaches 300 mg/l and continues to climb to as high as 1320 mg/l just below the confluence of the San Joaquin and Merced Rivers.

Irrigated agriculture is particularly threatened by high soil salinity in areas with poor drainage. Many parts of the Central Valley have saline water tables near the surface, and on-farm subsurface tile drains can cost from $100 to $700 per acre. Often, the economic value of crop production does not justify the cost. Alternatives for disposing of the saline water are also expensive: evaporation ponds may add $500 to $3000 per acre to on-farm drainage costs.

The Central Valley's other water quality problem is the high level of selenium, a toxic element, in drainage water. Naturally occurring selenium deposits underlying irrigated soils are leached out during irrigation and then concentrated to toxic levels when irrigation return flows drain into the marshes of local wildlife preserves. Public concern over the dying and deformed birds of the Kesterson Wildlife Refuge has underscored the need to solve this problem. Toxic return flows plague other U.S. Bureau of Reclamation projects in the West as well. Solutions will not be easy to effect since the irrigators themselves do not suffer the damages and thus resist any regulation of return flows.

Meanwhile, the supplier of all federal water in the Central Valley, the Bureau of Reclamation, is under considerable pressure to change its longstanding policy of subsidizing irrigation. The new rules of the Reclamation Reform Act of 1982 limiting subsidies are being fought by big irrigation districts' lobbyists, sometimes successfully.[36] The vested economic and political power of the Central Valley's large farms and irrigation districts present a challenge to those who want subsidies to irrigation removed. However, the growing awareness of water scarcity on the part of urban residents, who make up the bulk of California's populace, signals a new level of debate.

The High Plains of Texas

Irrigated agriculture on the High Plains of Texas is predicated on the mining of the underlying Ogallala aquifer.[37] (See Figure 5.) The problems that agriculture faces on the High Plains are not caused by the proximity of growing urban areas; nor are they problems of water quality. Instead, the ongoing and unsustainable overdraft of mostly fossil water will ultimately lead to a cessation of irrigation on the High Plains.

Cotton (34 percent of harvested acres during 1971–1982), wheat (25 percent), grain sorghum (23 percent), and corn (8 percent) are the crops most often grown on the High Plains, although about half the land is pasture or rangeland. Approximately half of all the cropland is irrigated with groundwater from the Ogallala aquifer.

> The vested economic and political power of the Central Valley's large farms and irrigation districts present a challenge to those who want subsidies to irrigation removed. However, the growing awareness of water scarcity on the part of urban residents, who make up the bulk of California's populace, signals a new level of debate.

27

Dryland farming accounts for the other half of cropland in this semi-arid climate.

Each year, between five and eight million acre-feet of water are drawn from the Ogallala, while recharge is negligible in most areas, averaging only 372,000 acre-feet. By 1980, approximately 23 percent of the Ogallala in Texas had been mined, a total of 110 million acre-feet extracted from an

---

Figure 5: The Ogallala Aquifer In The Southern High Plains Of Texas

---

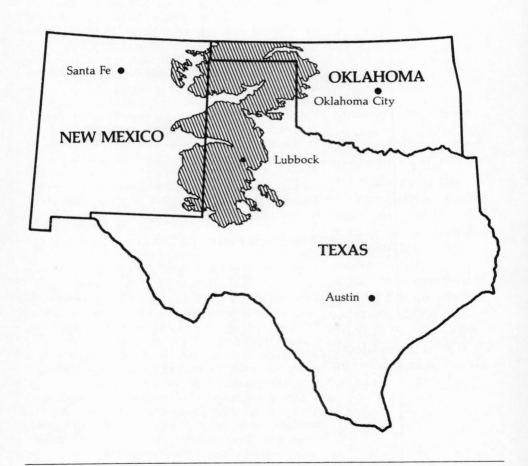

Source: High Plains Associates, *Six-State High Plains-Ogallala Aquifer Regional Resources Study*, A Report To The U.S. Department of Commerce and the High Plains Study Council (March 1982) p. 2-3

initial supply of 500 million acre-feet. Inevitably, mining diminishes the saturated thickness of the aquifer and increases pumping depths. Because energy for pumping is the largest component of water costs in the region, irrigation water expenses have risen substantially with increases in the real cost of energy over the last fifteen years and with the increased pumping lifts.

In the short term, farmers can adjust to higher water costs by switching to those crops that require less irrigation water or that produce a higher economic return to water, adopting more efficient irrigation technologies and water-management schemes, and returning some acreage to dryland production. Evidence of these adjustments can already be found. As Figure 6 shows, total acreage does not appear to be decreasing rapidly (although the total number of farms decreased over the same period), but there is a clear trend toward dryland farming. Specifically, while total cotton acreage has increased steadily, dryland production has grown twice as fast as irrigated production. Clearly, the transition from irrigated to dryland crop production is under way in this region of the High Plains.

Over the longer term, efficient irrigation technologies can prolong the Ogallala aquifer's life, but they are expensive to install. For the most part, farmers lack the expertise and the capital needed for these investments, though state and federal agricultural extension programs are natural vehicles for information dissemination.

The long-term result of aquifer mining, given the paucity of other water-supply options, will be a continuing shift to dryland farming and land abandonment. Despite some promising enhanced-recovery experiments, with the aquifer yielding water at about $50 per acre-foot, it is clear that the intensive cropping of rangeland with water from the Ogallala will continue to decline. As the transition to dryland farming accelerates accordingly, an increase in monoculture cropping (especially of cotton), with attendant soil erosion and nutrient depletion, is likely. The sandy soils of the High Plains are particularly vulnerable to wind erosion in the absence of a cover provided by crop residues or growing crops. Indeed, converting from irrigation to dryland farming could increase soil erosion rates by 100 percent. Where top soils are shallow, increased levels of erosion could sap

Converting from irrigation to dryland farming could increase soil erosion rates by 100 percent.

productivity and usher in a return of the dust bowl conditions of the 1930s. These dire predictions can, however, be tempered by policies that encourage the reestablishment of vegetation to protect the fragile soils.

Federal and state cost-sharing programs for soil and water conservation have existed for many

---

Figure 6: Acreage Of Major Crops Harvested, 3-Year Moving Averages, Southern High Plains Of Texas: 1973-1982

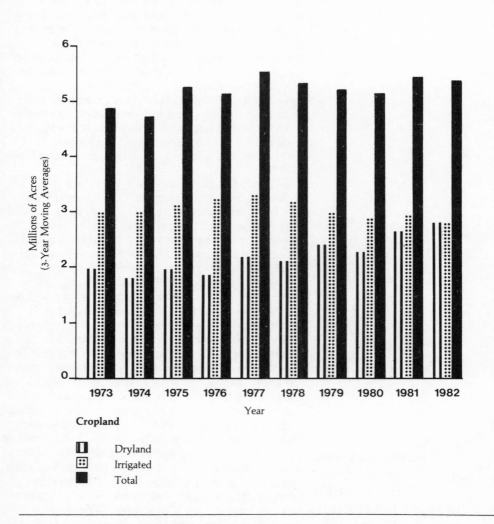

years. But most facilitate ongoing irrigation, not land retirement. For example, a Texas law provides for low-interest loans to farmers to purchase efficient irrigation equipment. However, recent federal legislation in the 1985 Farm Bill may reduce soil erosion through a long-term ''conservation reserve'' program under which highly erodible land can be taken out of production. Under this program, the U.S. Department of Agriculture (USDA) will share with farmers the costs of establishing a vegetative cover to reduce wind and water erosion. The program's current goal is to retire 45 million acres nationwide by 1990, although initial results suggest that USDA price-support programs may be undermining the land retirement program.[38]

The Upper Colorado River Basin

The Colorado River Compact apportions the flows of the Colorado between the states of the Upper and Lower Basins.[39] Like the prior appropriation doctrine practiced in most western states, the Colorado River apportionment dictates that if a state cannot use all the water to which it is entitled, the right to use that water goes to the next ''senior'' appropriator. At present, because economic development in the Upper Basin has lagged behind that in the Lower Basin, the unused water is being used in the Lower Basin.

Theoretically, the Upper Basin states have reserved rights to their apportioned flows and these rights can be developed whenever water is needed. In practice, however, cities and industries in the Lower Basin depend increasingly on the Upper Basin's unused outflows. Partly out of a belief that they should develop their rights before it is too late, the Upper Basin states are now taking the path of preemptive development. All too often, they promote water projects that are economically and environmentally unjustifiable. Many such projects are designed to supply water uses that are of low value or little demand.

Irrigation is the number one water consumer in the Upper Basin. The economic return to consumptive water use in irrigation is relatively low, on the order of $10 to $25 per acre-foot in the Upper Basin. Indirect income from activity in the agricultural sector, however, indicates that the state economies derive additional value from irrigated crop production—one reason why

> Out of a belief that they should develop their rights before it is too late, the Upper Basin states are now taking the path of preemptive development.

Colorado plans to increase irrigated acreage in its western counties.

On average, an estimated 2.89 million acre-feet (maf) of water, in excess of compact-required outflows of 8.25 maf (7.5 maf plus half of the United States' obligation to Mexico of 1.5 maf), flow out of the Upper Basin unused each year. These flows produce recreational opportunities and generate hydroelectric power as they travel down to Arizona and California, where they are finally used for irrigation and for residential, commercial, and industrial needs. Clearly, the return to consumptive water use in agriculture in the Upper Basin is less than the return to the instream and offstream uses of the same water in the Lower Basin. Yet, the benefits of Upper Basin outflows accrue to the Lower Basin states—in the form of lower electricity costs, better water quality, and eventual offstream returns—with no sharing of the bounty with the Upper Basin states. In the meantime, Upper Basin states encourage agriculture to expand water use because doing so generates economic activity and income at home.

This complicated story is further embellished by the consideration of water quality. Irrigation return flows in the Upper Basin add salts to the river, increasing its salinity. Without a salinity control program, the salinity of the Colorado River at Imperial Dam may reach 1100 mg/l in 2010. In addition, through evaporation and transpiration, irrigation in the Upper Basin consumes vast quantities of pristine headwaters— waters that, if left in the river, could dilute much of the salt added to the river as it flows along its lengthy course. Thus, through both loading and concentration, irrigation in the Upper Basin contributes to the salinization of the Colorado River.

In a sense, developing and using Colorado River water to irrigate low-valued crops in the Upper Basin is a double insult: the total basin-wide economic return to water could be increased if more of it were allowed to flow downstream to be used eventually in the Lower Basin, and the salinity problem would decline. But the rules of the Colorado River Compact provide absolutely no incentive for such a shift. Since the Upper Basin states do not "own" their shares of the river, but have rights only to use them, arrangements to sell or lease water to Lower Basin entities are difficult. Not that efforts have not been attempted: when the potential gain is great, entrepreneurs will act. The Galloway Group in Colorado has attempted to develop unused rights in Colorado for sale to San Diego, and the legal verdict is still out.

At present, there are no mechanisms for managing the Colorado River Basin as a whole. Increasingly, agriculture in the Upper Basin is eyed by the thirsty cities in the Lower Basin. And as the economic values of water use shift, changes in the balance of power cannot be far behind. The dilemma of the Colorado River is an interstate one, but it mirrors the growing conflict between agricultural and urban water users within the individual states.

The dilemma of the Colorado River is an interstate one, but it mirrors the growing conflict between agricultural and urban water users within the individual states.

V. The Cities and Water

The municipal sector is the fastest-growing water user in the West.[40] Since municipal water demand is partly a function of the population level, the growth in population in the West in the last two decades is illuminating. As Table 3 shows, the number of inhabitants in western cities has increased tremendously since 1960. Although the rate of population growth in the West appears to have slowed in recent years, the number of residents continues to rise and forecasts call for increases well beyond the year 2000. While water use by the municipal sector is small compared to the agricultural sector, municipal use sometimes reaches 10 percent of total consumption. *(See Table 4.)*

Municipal water use comprises numerous distinctly different demands that can be loosely categorized as residential, public, and commercial. Residential or household demand consists of such outdoor uses as lawn irrigation, car washing, or evaporative cooling, and such indoor uses as bathing or cooking. Public use includes firefighting and maintenance of public buildings and grounds. Commercial and light industrial demands are often met through a municipal water delivery system and are thus included in most municipal data on water demand.

Much of the water cities use is not actually consumed.

Much of the water cities use is not actually consumed in the process. Water used indoors for bathing, cooking, and washing is not consumed, though its quality becomes degraded. Water used outdoors for lawn irrigation, on the other hand, is largely consumed since it evaporates, seeps into the ground, or is lost to the evapotranspiration of plants. Also, evaporative air conditioning units

Table 3. Population Growth in Selected Cities of the Western United States

City	Population (thousands)			Percentage Change	
	1960	1970	1980	1960–1970	1970–1980
Albuquerque, New Mexico	276	333	454	20.7	36.3
Denver-Boulder, Colorado	935	1240	1620	32.6	30.6
El Paso, Texas	314	359	480	14.3	33.7
Las Vegas, Nevada	127	273	462	115.0	69.2
Los Angeles-Anaheim-Long Beach, California	7752	9981	11496	28.8	15.2
Phoenix, Arizona	664	971	1508	46.2	55.3
Salt Lake City, Utah	576	705	936	22.4	32.8
San Diego, California	1033	1358	1862	31.5	37.1
Tucson, Arizona	266	352	531	32.3	50.9

Source: U.S. Department of Commerce, Bureau of Census, *Statistical Abstracts of the United States-1981* (Washington, D.C., United States Government Printing Office, December 1981) pp. 18–20.

consume large quantities of water in climates where relative humidity is low, as it is in Arizona. Including all municipal water uses, the percentage of consumption to withdrawal averages 25 percent across the country.[41] In arid locales where outdoor water use and air conditioning water use comprise a larger fraction of total usage, the percentage is higher.[42] In Denver, for example, 51 percent of municipal water supply is used to water lawns—a use that accounts for 94 percent of water consumption in the city.[43]

Municipal water demand is influenced by a number of factors. One is season: outdoor irrigation of lawns and urban parks and the use of water-cooled air conditioners cause the average

Table 4. Municipal Water Use

	Consumptive Use in 1980 (million gallons/day)	Percentage of Total Consumptive Use
Arizona	340	8
California	1700	7
Colorado	160	4
Nevada	69	4
New Mexico	99	5
Texas	640	6
Utah	300	10

Source: U.S. Geological Survey, *National Water Summary 1983-Hydrologic Events and Issues,* Water Supply Paper No. 2,250 (Washington, D.C., U.S. Government Printing Office, 1984).

In general, per capita municipal use is higher in the arid West than anywhere else in the country.

monthly water consumption to more than double in the hot summer months. Other factors are the number of residents per water meter and the household income level: the more people per household and the more water-intensive amenities (such as swimming pools) they can afford, the greater the household water demand. Communities with higher per capita income usually have more commercial establishments per resident and more public facilities (such as golf courses) requiring irrigation, and thus have higher per capita water demand profiles. Another factor is population density: where households are clustered in apartment buildings, lawns and gardens are smaller, and so per capita outdoor water use is lower. In general, per capita municipal use is higher in the arid West than anywhere else in the country. For example, average summer household use in Raleigh, North Carolina (1973) was 8.81 hundred cubic feet per month while average summer household use in Tucson, Arizona (1979) was 16.43.[44] This striking difference reflects the extensive irrigation of both residential and public landscaping in Arizona and the ubiquitous use of water-cooled air conditioning in the hot, dry climate.

Many economic studies confirm the general impression that municipal water use does respond to changes in price, although it is termed inelastic because a 10-percent rise in price triggers less than a 10-percent decrease in overall demand.

Price is another determinant of water demand. Many economic studies confirm the general impression that municipal water use does respond to changes in price, although it is termed inelastic because a 10-percent rise in price triggers less than a 10-percent decrease in overall demand. Compelling evidence indicates that so-called outdoor water uses are much more price sensitive (or elastic) than in-house uses.[45]

Water for municipal use is most often supplied by an urban water department, public water utility, or water conservation district that acts as a broker for the consumers. These water service agencies and districts may own appropriative surface rights or may have contracted for federal or state project water. In addition, many own their own wells. There may be several organizational levels between the holder of the water right and the consumer, including water wholesalers, distributors, and retailers.

The ultimate consumers, the households, are supplied with pressurized, treated water delivered to the tap on demand, a service for which the providing agency charges according to a rate structure. Most towns have residential water meters and charge a flat rate plus a "block use" charge that goes down with successive increments of use. In general, urban water rates are designed to give price breaks to large water users and to cover the provider's costs exactly (average cost pricing). By law, publicly owned utilities are not generally allowed to make profits, and average cost pricing is one way to ensure that revenues exactly cover costs. Some cities have a large number of unmetered residences. In Denver, Colorado, for instance, 88,000 residences are without meters.[46] These municipalities may instead charge a toll based on the assessed value of the property or exact a flat fee for water and sewer service.

By and large, the pricing practices of most cities eliminate incentives to conserve water.

By and large, the pricing practices of most cities eliminate incentives to conserve water. To most consumers, the water bill amounts to a very small line item in a monthly budget—perhaps one reason water demand studies often show a small price response at current prices. Were water rates to rise, demand might be more price-sensitive. At present levels of water consumption, the marginal value of water for household use is surprisingly small: in other words, most households would be willing to forego significant amounts of ordinary water usage (especially summertime outdoor usage) if the financial incentive existed. With greater scarcity, however, the value of water for household use can be almost infinite. As inessential uses are cut back, the remaining water usage becomes quite valuable to the consumer, confirming the general perception that water for basic human needs represents the highest legal priority and receives the greatest security of supply.

Since population expansion and the growth of associated support industries continue apace in the West, procuring water supplies for cities looms as a major political priority. Forecasts of population growth in the West imply that water demand will also grow, even if per capita use remains the same or falls slightly. (Perhaps erroneously, most forecasters of growth assume that water resources will continue to be a bargain in the region.)

As cities grow and water service agencies face ever-increasing demands, they cast about for new supplies. Among the options available to the city, appropriating surface water or drilling new wells for groundwater are less and less tenable. Sometimes a city, such as Tucson, can condemn or annex surrounding agricultural lands and take over the water rights previously used in irrigation or buy agricultural water rights outright. Leasing or exchange agreements can also increase the effective yield of a water system. Alternatively, the city may construct new water storage and importation projects, most often with some financial backing from the state or the federal governments. However, faced with shrinking budgets and rising construction costs, cities are finding large storage projects less attractive. Which options are available to the specific urban area depends in large measure on the local and regional geography and on the water laws and institutions of the particular state.[47]

Most urban water management agencies behave conservatively. In other words, their objective is to develop supplies to meet anticipated demand, whatever that might be. Most water managers, either elected or appointed, believe that their mandate is to ensure that the city has secure, plentiful, and low-cost supplies and that revenues exactly cover the costs of water services. Few water service agencies attempt to control water demand through pricing, and few take a stand on urban growth. Clearly, however, land-use planning, density zoning, and taxation are tools for urban growth control at the hands of a city council or other planning agency, and decisions on these matters affect future urban water demand.

Since they believe their mandate is to meet rather than control demand, water service agencies act defensively, undertaking preemptive development to maximize supplies for urban growth far into the future. Acquisitions and projects are usually financed through municipal bonds or special taxes since a dependable water supply is viewed as an asset to all citizens, regardless of how much water each personally uses. Through rate structures and financing methods, the entities that supply western cities with water have ensured that household consumers never face the marginal cost of their use. In addition, citizens have few opportunities or incentives to involve themselves in decision-making.

When droughts befall a city, the usual management strategies are to educate and cajole the public into cooperation and to restrict specific water uses through such measures as alternate-day lawn watering or a ban on car-washing. Since most utilities design the water-delivery system to meet peak summer afternoon demand, these measures ameliorate the effects of drought by shaving the peak demand. Yet, in procuring reliable water supplies and planning for the future demand of a metropolitan area, few cities consider the wisdom of adapting water demand measures on a regular basis. At current rates of consumption, expanding the system's capacity almost always costs more than the value of the marginal uses the expansion is intended to meet.

Through rate structures and financing methods, the entities that supply western cities with water have ensured that household consumers never face the marginal cost of their use.

VI. Case Studies of Municipal Water Demand

The South Coast Basin of California

California's South Coast Basin, which includes Los Angeles and San Diego, as well as numerous urban and suburban communities, is the world's largest urban area dependent upon imported water.[48] Mean annual precipitation in the region is only 14 inches, with a variation between 5 and 38 inches over the period of record. This rainfall is seasonal, falling mostly between November and April.

The region's modern history has been characterized by the development of supplemental water supplies and storage facilities needed to regulate water flows and redress the natural imbalance between periods of peak supply and peak demand. Three major aqueducts and their associated storage reservoirs permit the South Coast Basin to import California-allocated water from the Colorado River, State Water Project water from the Central Valley of California, and appropriated groundwater pumped in the Owens Valley to the northeast.

The development of remote water supplies made explosive population growth in the South Coast Basin possible. Since 1940 alone, the Basin's population has grown from 2.9 million to well over 12 million, and this growth is expected to continue, although at lower rates. Averaging 10 percent annually, this dramatic population increase has been fueled by many factors, including the favorable climate and the rise of defense and aerospace-related industries. The Metropolitan Water District of Southern California

(MWD), the region's principal water wholesaler, projects that regional population will grow by about 34 percent between 1980 and 2000, a total increase of a little over 4 million. According to MWD projections, this population growth will increase water demand from 3.06 million acre-feet (maf) in 1980 to 3.61 maf in 2000. (To arrive at this estimate, MWD considered the population growth projection and adjusted current per capita use rates for the effects of conservation and education programs, sociological shifts in water use patterns, and lowered industrial demand after the imposition of increased sewer charges.)

Arrayed against the demand estimates is a water supply system that encompasses water entitlements and delivery capabilities totalling 4.79 maf, three quarters of which comes from remote sources through the Colorado River Aqueduct, the Los Angeles Aqueduct, and the State Water Project. These entitlements, however, have been eroded by legal and political developments over the last three decades. MWD can no longer count on its historical quantity of water from the Colorado River, as Arizona reclaims its share for the Central Arizona Project. In fact, 495,000 acre-feet is the MWD's current firm allocation from the Colorado River, taking into account recent Indian awards.

The magnitude of the City of Los Angeles' supplies from the Owens Valley and the Mono Lake Basin is also in question. Owens Valley has challenged Los Angeles' rights to pump groundwater, filing a lawsuit and forcing reduced pumping rates for environmental reasons. In a novel move, the Public Trust Doctrine was invoked on behalf of the interests of Mono Lake Basin. Water taken by the Los Angeles Water Department (LAWD) from inflows to Mono Lake has lowered the lake and increased its salinity so much that bird populations are threatened both by a drop in food (brine shrimp cannot tolerate high salinity levels) and by natural predators that can reach nesting islands by newly exposed land bridges. When settled, the lawsuits initiated by environmental groups could drastically lower the amount of water LAWD is allowed to remove from the Mono Lake Basin.

Besides pending lawsuits, political obstacles also threaten MWD's entitlements. Completing segments of the California State Water Project could eliminate the projected gap between supply and demand, but at enormous cost. MWD's firm entitlement from the SWP (2.01 maf) depends on the construction of additional conveyance and storage projects that have not garnered the necessary political support. Currently, only 1.13 maf of dependable supply can be counted on from the SWP. Thus, MWD estimates that its total firm supply in normal years could be only 3.47 maf in 2000, not including the effects of legislation pending in the Owens Valley-Mono Lake controversies. Apparently, supplies are inadequate to meet the projected growth in water demand between now and 2000 at current per capita use rates.

MWD has exercised care in testing the sensitivity of its demand forecasts to various assumptions about population growth and climatic variation. But it does not acknowledge the possibility that the price of water could affect the quantities demanded, even though increases in the cost of energy needed to convey imported water will be reflected in water prices as early as 1986. Moreover, new supply facilities will cost significantly more than existing ones. Although these higher costs are rolled into water prices under an average cost pricing system, marginal cost pricing would certainly affect water demand noticeably. By some estimates, average cost pricing policies would cause water demand in the MWD to be 8.4 percent more in 2000 and 10 percent more in 2020 than it would be under marginal cost pricing policies.

Like many urban areas in the West, California's South Coast Basin is casting about for new supplies to satisfy projected demands and make up the shortfall from lost historical sources of supply. But the alternatives are limited.

Like many urban areas in the West, California's South Coast Basin is casting about for new supplies to satisfy projected demands and make up the shortfall from lost historical sources of supply. But the alternatives are limited. The SWP additions are expensive and whether the beneficiaries of the new supplies would be willing, on the margin, to pay for them is open to question. Recently, the MWD began approaching other water users, namely the Imperial Irrigation District, hoping to purchase, lease, or salvage additional water supplies. The MWD proposed to pay Imperial Irrigation District $10 million annually to fund studies and water-conservation projects, the water savings from which (estimated at 100,000 acre-feet annually) would go to the MWD.

Tucson, Arizona

Arizona is one of the most arid states in the country. Rainfall is sparse, seasonal, and concentrated mostly in the Central Highlands Province.[49] *(See Figure 7.)* This central region—which gets 10 to 35 inches of rain per year—is Arizona's principal source of perennial water supply, providing streamflow and groundwater recharge to the Desert Lowlands Province to the south. Only small quantities of precipitation fall within the Desert Lowlands Province itself, and then mostly during summer thunderstorms. Evaporation, transpiration, and percolation claim most of the 11 inches of precipitation that falls, on average, in the Tucson area. Thus, this city has turned to large stores of underground water that have accumulated over centuries in the sand and gravel of the partially filled valleys. Since at least the early 1940s, the rate of withdrawal has been far greater than the rate of recharge to the aquifer.

Like most sunbelt cities, Tucson has grown phenomenally in the last few decades. Its appeal lies in its natural setting, ringed by mountains and beautiful desert on all sides, and in the warm, dry, and sunny climate. Estimates indicate that the population of the Tucson Active Management Area (AMA, consisting of Tucson and the surrounding agricultural lands) will nearly triple from its 1986 level of 0.62 million to 1.59 million people by 2025. Seventy-five percent of that growth is projected to come from in-migration.

About 80 percent of Tucson's water supply comes from groundwater pumped in well-fields in and south of the city along the dry Santa Cruz riverbed. The balance is pumped from retired agricultural land in neighboring valleys and conveyed through the Tucson Mountains. Average yearly pumpage over 1975–1980 was 179,000 acre-feet for municipal, industrial, and mining needs and 230,000 acre-feet for irrigation. The groundwater overdraft for 1975–1980 averaged 79 percent of total consumptive use. *(See Figure 8).*

Clearly, Tucson cannot continue indefinitely with this pattern of water consumption. In fact, the innovative Arizona Groundwater Management Act forces the Tucson AMA to achieve zero groundwater overdraft by 2025. The scheduled arrival of water supplies from the Central Arizona Project (CAP) by 1992 will help forestall inevitable sacrifices, but that welcome infusion alone cannot save the Tucson AMA from water shortages if current use patterns continue. Given expected levels of urban growth and per

Figure 7: Water Provinces Of Arizona

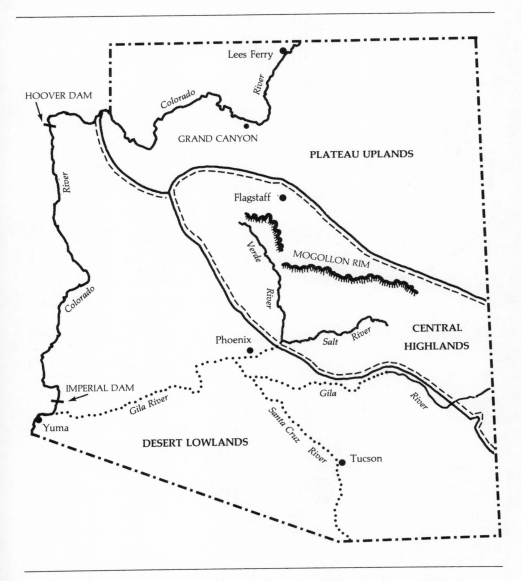

Source: Adapted from Jack L. Cross, Elizabeth H. Shaw, and Kathleen Scheifle, eds. *Arizona, Its People And Resources* (Tucson: University of Arizona Press, 1960)

45

Figure 8: Tucson's Water Balance

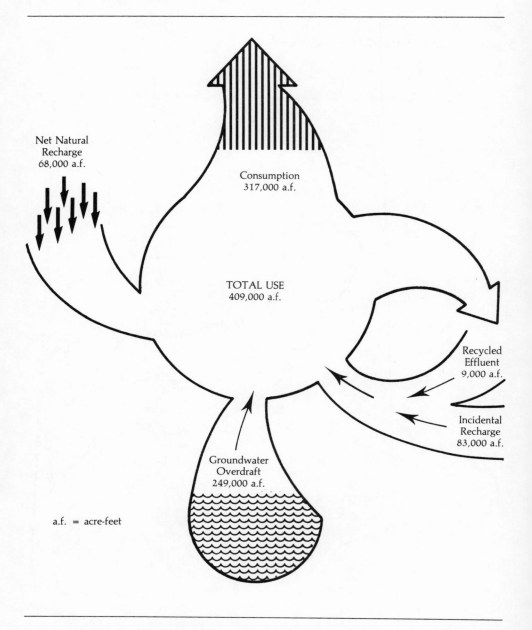

Net Natural
Recharge
68,000 a.f.

Consumption
317,000 a.f.

TOTAL USE
409,000 a.f.

Recycled
Effluent
9,000 a.f.

Incidental
Recharge
83,000 a.f.

Groundwater
Overdraft
249,000 a.f.

a.f. = acre-feet

Source: From data in William E. Martin, Helen M. Ingram, Dennis C. Cory, and Mary Wallace, "Toward Sustaining a Desert Metropolis: Water and Land Use In Tucson, Arizona," draft paper for the World Resources Institute (April 1986) p. 20

capita water-use rates, the projected water supply and water use budget for 2025 hangs in precarious balance. Achieving zero overdraft will require several additional controversial steps.

Demand management through higher water prices has a long and colorful history in Tucson. When Tucson's impending water-supply squeeze prompted several city council members to raise rates dramatically, they were promptly replaced with officials more sympathetic to the consumer's pocketbook. Currently, Tucson uses average cost pricing with an inverted block structure, based on a water cost of about $45 per acre-foot, and plans are to roll in the new, higher cost of the Central Arizona Project supplies. The price of CAP water charged Tucson will be subsidized by the federal government and the state: actual costs to deliver raw CAP water to Tucson will be about $100 per acre-foot, while the price for Tucson in the early years will be only $58 per acre-foot. Treating CAP water to the quality standards already met by groundwater would raise the real cost of CAP water to around $250 per acre-foot.

Per capita water use in Tucson appears to have dropped since higher rates were imposed in 1974. From a high of 205 gallons per capita per day (gcd) in 1973–74, pumpage averaged 153 gcd from 1976 to 1984. A change in pricing to marginal cost pricing would undoubtedly have further, dramatic effects.

In another effort to keep supply and demand balanced, Tucson buys and retires agricultural lands, keeping the grandfathered consumptive water rights for the city. But the environmental consequences of land abandonment are startling: these lands do not return to virgin desert, but are subject to erosion. Nonetheless, urban water demand is swelling and the city can afford to buy agricultural lands. The numbers are disputed, but Tucson believes water enough for many decades of growth underlies the Avra and Altar Valleys to the east. Even this option is limited, though, since only 58 percent of water in the Tucson AMA is currently consumed in agriculture (compared to a 90-percent state average).

Another step toward balancing supply and demand is recycling urban water, a controversial topic. At present, municipal effluent is used to irrigate public parks and golf courses. If the anticipated population growth materializes, Tucson will have to reuse its entire effluent if the

When Tucson's impending water-supply squeeze prompted several city council members to raise rates dramatically, they were promptly replaced with officials more sympathetic to the consumer's pocketbook.

AMA is to reach its goal of zero groundwater overdraft in 2025, while maintaining an agricultural sector.

This bleak picture of Tucson's future need not be a prediction, however. If the environmental amenities that draw so many people to Tucson are destroyed by phenomenal urban growth, the forecasted levels of growth may not materialize. Likewise, Tucsonans might come to realize that their desert environment can support only a certain population and decide to limit growth. Water demand management could also relieve much of the pressure on supplies by lowering per capita consumption.

Finally, it also seems logical that desert farming could succumb to economic or political pressures and, except for some irrigated agriculture on Indian lands, could cease in the Tucson AMA. If all crop irrigation in the region apart from that on reservations were eliminated, Tucson could balance its water budget in 2025 without resorting to across-the-board reductions in use in other sectors. If a water market were allowed to operate, irrigated agriculture on Indian lands would probably decline as well, since water sold to Tucson would fetch more money than it would be worth in crop production.

Denver, Colorado

Denver, situated where two streams meet in the semi-arid South Platte River Valley, receives an annual average of 14 inches of precipitation, mostly from winter snows.[50] The city's water supply comes from locally developed groundwater and surface water, including the Platte River, and water imported from the western side of the Rocky Mountains through the Continental Divide. Currently, the total metropolitan water supply totals 418,000 acre-feet safe annual yield, of which 295,000 is in the Denver Water Department system. Most of the water, 84 percent, comes from surface sources.

Denver's population has grown rapidly since World War II, primarily from migration spurred by an appealing climate, recreational opportunities, and jobs. The current population of the metropolitan area is 1.8 million people, and forecasts of future urban growth diverge widely. The middle road suggests that growth will continue, though at a lower rate than in the 1960s

If the environmental amenities that draw so many people to Tucson are destroyed by phenomenal urban growth, the forecasted levels of growth may not materialize. Likewise, Tucsonans might come to realize that their desert environment can support only a certain population and decide to limit growth.

and 1970s, and that the metropolitan population will reach about 3 million people by 2010. Already, urban expansion can be seen all along the eastern edge of the front range of the Rocky Mountains, from Fort Collins to the north to Colorado Springs to the south.

Current water supplies cannot support Denver's officially forecast population much past 1990. But the citizenry is divided on how best to plan for future water needs. The Denver Water Department is aggressively pursuing an additional storage and regulatory reservoir (Two Forks Project) on the South Platte River that could increase the safe annual yield of the Denver system by up to 98,000 acre-feet, at a cost of about $300 million. But concern over the project's environmental impacts and a belief that less costly alternatives exist have caused fierce opposition to Two Forks. Suburban water agencies are also considering several transmountain water-importation projects, including compensatory storage reservoirs on the western slope, although the costs—in the range of $10,000 per acre-foot of safe yield—are becoming prohibitive even for supplying municipal water needs.

Water diverted from agriculture could serve as a source of water supply for Denver and its suburbs. However, water transfers in Colorado are handled by water courts, and the transaction costs of legal proceedings and information gathering are high. Irrigators can transfer only as much water as was consumptively used on the farm, and often the court's findings are conservative. Nonetheless, water has been transferred from farms to cities in many cases. For instance, purchases of agricultural water by Aurora (a Denver suburb) and Colorado Springs over the last 24 years have caused irrigated acreage in Crowley County in the Arkansas Valley to decline by 35 percent.

To reduce opposition to the Two Forks Project, the city of Denver has announced its intent to install water meters in the 88,000 still-unmetered residential homes. However, pricing programs and demand management in general have received little attention. One obstacle is the setting for water management in the metropolitan area: Denver is surrounded by a set of acrimonious and uncooperative suburban water service agencies. Without their joint and concerted efforts, water development, pricing, and demand management will continue on a haphazard path. If they had a

Pricing programs and demand management in general have received little attention.

unified water service agency, the city of Denver and the suburban communities could collectively manage their water supplies and maximize yields. With the present fragmented approach, some agencies hold excess supplies while others remain dangerously reliant on limited supplies. Many communities with self-protective attitudes offer cheaper water to those ''in the fold,'' which works against effective demand management. The rift is real and divisive: metered customers in the City and County of Denver pay an average of $176 per year for water while suburban total-service customers pay double that, or $350 per year.

VII. Emerging Conflicts and Policy Recommendations

From any close look at the major demands on western water resources emerges a sense of the inevitability of conflict. Evidence of pressure on water is everywhere since most streams and rivers in the West have been fully appropriated. Salinity and toxic elements threaten traditional agricultural practices and impose high costs on subsequent water users. Groundwater that is tributary to a watercourse usually cannot be tapped without coincident retirement of surface flow rights, and non-tributary groundwater is being mined at high rates. In fact, use exceeds average streamflow in nearly every western subregion, and the deficits are being offset with groundwater and imported water from adjoining basins. *(See Figure 9.)*

Use exceeds average streamflow in nearly every western sub-region, and the deficits are being offset with groundwater and imported water from adjoining basins.

Several major cities in the Southwest, including Tucson, are now mining groundwater aquifers to meet normal demand. Reliable yields from these sources are falling, and economic exhaustion will soon be approached. Other cities, such as Los Angeles, face a reduction in long-held supplies as upstream states claim their Compact-apportioned shares of Colorado River water. As cities attempt to increase supplies to meet growing demands, instream flows may be diminished and water use in other offstream sectors may be politically, if not legally, threatened. The conflicts over water supplies and water quality degradation are not limited to a particular state, but thrive in every state in the West and even extend across state borders.

51

Although the focus here is on water demand in the municipal and agricultural sectors, the overall competition for water supplies in the West has been growing as strong demands emerge in other sectors as well. The "energy sector" is perceived as a new rival to traditional water users in the West, although the economic viability of unsubsidized synfuels development is nil. Recreational demand for water has grown along with population growth, and the value placed on instream flow for fishing, swimming, and boating has increased accordingly. When populations expand and urban areas sprawl, remaining

Figure 9: Groundwater Overdraft

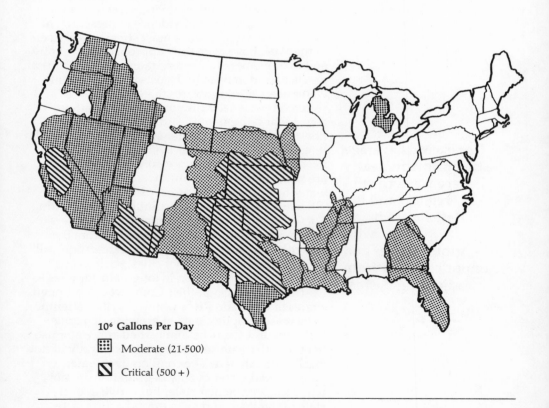

10⁶ Gallons Per Day

▦ Moderate (21-500)

◪ Critical (500 +)

Source: Ernest A. Engelbert with Ann Foley Scheuring, eds., *Water Scarcity* (Berkeley: University of California Press, 1984) p. 28

wilderness areas and the water flowing through them also become more precious as legacies for future generations. Particularly on rivers developed to generate hydroelectric power, the economic value of water left flowing in the river can be quite high. Similarly, as salinity levels reach new highs in the major rivers, the instream value of pristine water for dilution rises.[51]

The competition for water supplies is perhaps most obvious between cities and farms. Irrigated agriculture uses the most water of any activity in the West, yet this use is often inefficient, largely because policies and laws discourage conservation. While irrigated agriculture has held a favored position in water allocation for decades, and farms hold many of the senior appropriative water rights, urban water demands have grown rapidly and citizens of the arid West intend to keep their oases green. When urban water managers eye the volumes of water used in irrigation, using words like "waste," farmers' animosity toward the cities grows. Irrigators want to keep their supplies, especially if subsidized, or realize an economic gain for forfeiting their water rights or investing in water-use efficiency. Naturally, those "holding the cards" in uncertain times have a substantial advantage, so irrigation districts often prefer to retain their rights even when offered what appears to be a good deal—witness the Imperial Irrigation District's recent rejection of an initial offer from the Metropolitan Water District.[52] Nonetheless, thirsty cities, eager to secure supplies, can lobby for new definitions of "reasonable use" in agriculture or condemn agricultural water rights outright in many states. Without an increase in available water supplies, active water markets, or some equitable adjustment in the rules governing the allocation and reallocation of resources, pressures on water resources will only mount.

For many reasons, historical strategies for increasing surface supplies by capturing excess stream flows and constructing storage facilities are approaching obsolescence. First, the optimal reservoir locations have been developed, and construction of new storage shows diminishing marginal returns. Remaining sites are suitable for smaller dams and present engineering challenges that are inevitably expensive. Costs for all types of capital construction are up, and to add to the financial constraints, federal funds for large water projects are drying up in an age of fiscal austerity.

While irrigated agriculture has held a favored position in water allocation for decades, urban water demands have grown rapidly and citizens of the arid West intend to keep their oases green.

53

New formulas for cost-sharing between the federal and state governments will probably ensure that a greater percentage of the financial burden is borne by the states in the future. Finally, a new alliance of budget-cutters and environmentalists has focused attention on the full costs of new dams, including the loss of free-flowing river reaches and the inundation of fertile lands and the habitats of fish and wildlife. Even small-scale municipal reservoir projects that might pass the cost-benefit test face expensive legal battles over environmental impacts.

Proposals for interbasin transfers of water have met with the same resistance in recent years. Environmentalists point out the lost value of recreation sites and wildlife habitat, as well as the potential for ecological disruption, especially through the introduction of foreign aquatic species to a targeted watershed. Grandiose engineering feats still receive media attention, but most water managers now recognize that the costs are prohibitive and no longer take seriously such schemes as transferring water from the Great Lakes and Canada to Arizona and Texas. Finally, there are few river basins, even those with excess water today, whose inhabitants would let their supplies go to another geographic area without compensation. Basins-of-origin protection clauses in state laws may be used to ensure that potential exporting basins are rewarded.

The marginal cost of developing new increments of supply usually exceeds the marginal value of water in the use for which it is intended.

Another drawback of many proposed water projects is that the marginal cost of developing new increments of supply usually exceeds the marginal value of water in the use for which it is intended. Federal benefit-cost estimates for irrigation projects invariably include the secondary indirect benefits of reservoir construction and increased farming activity so as to show a positive ratio and justify a project. The marginal value of water in municipal use is not high enough to support many proposed projects for increasing urban supplies. Only when project costs are shifted—by drawing on general revenues rather than exposing costs directly through higher consumer water bills—do such projects receive wide public support.

Acceptance of the limitation of further supply-side thinking in water resources management is not universal, but when citizens are allowed to choose among alternatives, they often resoundingly reject large water projects.

Acceptance of the limitation of further supply-side thinking in water resources management is not universal, but when citizens are allowed to choose among alternatives, they often resoundingly reject large water projects. A combination of regional self-preservation on the part of the water-rich and a universal distaste for heavy taxes help

54

explain why. Recently, California voters elected to abandon plans for a north-south interbasin canal, the Peripheral Canal, suggesting that the historical pattern of moving more water from north to south in California will not continue.[53]

When choices for expanding usable supplies appear limited in the face of increasing competition, the alternative is to reduce demand for water. The future of western water use, as best it can be gleaned from conflicts emerging today, lies in conservation, improved efficiency, and reallocation of supplies among users and among sectors. All evidence indicates that the number of people living in the arid regions of the West will continue to rise. Barring a massive movement to halt or slow growth, a highly unlikely scenario, the carrying capacity of the region will be pushed to its limit, or at least that of its water supply. Arguably, the natural resources and environment of the West are already endangered by current development.

If the western states are to meet the future with prosperous economies, satisfied citizens, and an intact environment, policy change must be forthcoming. Unfortunately, the prior appropriation doctrine and the institutions designed to implement the laws stress the initial allocation of water supplies. Their usefulness for an orderly, effective, efficient, and ongoing reallocation process is under scrutiny in every state in the West. **Many observers believe that private property rights and free markets for water, like those for any other commodity, are needed.**[54] But it is not yet clear the extent to which the prior appropriation system can be modified and reinterpreted to allow water markets to operate effectively and fairly; nor has a consensus formed on the best ways to protect instream flows and water quality. Although the goal of improved water management appears simple enough, tremendous disagreement persists over the specific steps that should be taken.

Some change is already afoot. When economic pressures build and the marginal values of water use in different sectors diverge widely, institutions do evolve. Yet, too often, institutions change haphazardly for the sake of new powers—in the case of western water, urban interests. Although the greater play of competitive forces could help reallocate water to its most valuable uses, thereby increasing the total benefits of water use, the

55

challenge is to chart a path that does not ignore the consequences of transfers on third parties, and that does not stray far from protection of such public benefits as wildlife habitat, water quality, and instream flows for recreation.

Policy change aimed at increasing the efficiency of water use in different sectors, encouraging the movement of supplies from one use to another, and protecting the environment can take place at many levels. Managers of urban water agencies and irrigation districts must stretch their respective water budgets, and states must find ways to facilitate transfers among sectors. Also, the obvious void in interstate institutions for basin-wide water management challenges western states to find opportunities to cooperate and maximize benefits from water resources throughout the West.

Policies for Urban Water Service Agencies

Recent rapid rates of population growth in western cities have now slowed somewhat, but forecasts call for continued increases in the absolute number of people living and working in cities in the arid and semi-arid regions of the country. Simply appropriating new supplies is not an option for most of these cities, and the costs, both for construction and for legal fees, of importing new water supplies have become prohibitive. Given a limited water supply and a growing population, balancing water supply and demand will require new and creative approaches.

Temporarily leaving aside the question of buying or leasing existing water supplies from other sectors, the most viable option for cities attempting to satisfy growing water demand on a limited water budget is to reduce and restructure that demand, thus lowering per capita water use. **The most effective demand-curtailment program would contain elements of pricing, regulation, and education.** The "carrot and stick" approach to water management combines pricing water at its marginal cost to give consumers a clear idea of water scarcity with educating them on the need to reduce use and perhaps, rewarding them for water saved.

The key to the success of this policy package is setting water prices that do not obscure the marginal cost of providing water. Too often, the water service agency uses an average cost pricing formula to just cover the total costs of water service. But in many cases, a city's water supply curve exhibits large discontinuities. For example, Tucson currently mines good quality groundwater costing approximately $45 per acre-foot. But as groundwater mining is phased out, the city will have to turn to Central Arizona Project water that costs approximately $250 per acre-foot (excluding subsidies) by the time it is treated to bring it up to comparable quality.[55] Ideally, Tucsonans should pay the marginal cost of the new supplies, the CAP water, and thus base their consumption patterns on full knowledge of the cost of the next source of water. If water agencies are to maximize the benefits of resource use and allocate water efficiently, the marginal benefit of a consumer's water use should equal the marginal cost.

When average water costs are increasing, the use of average cost pricing rules creates an equilibrium characterized by lower prices and greater consumption when compared to the equilibrium under marginal cost pricing rules. *(See Figure 10.)* Clearly, imposing marginal cost pricing would dramatically affect total water demand in many cities. By one estimate, a change to marginal cost pricing in the Metropolitan Water District of Southern California would reduce demand by 260,000 acre-feet in 2000 and by 340,000 acre-feet in 2020; per capita use reductions would be small, amounting to 9 percent in 2000 and to 10 percent in 2020, and water prices would be 13.1 percent and 12.6 percent higher, respectively.[56] These figures illustrate how small changes in daily household use, 45 percent of which is for outdoor purposes in the MWD, can substantially change total water consumption within a basin.

Even with average cost pricing, the rate structure can make a difference. Traditionally, water is priced in declining block quantities: the more water a household uses, the less it costs for each successive increment. The odd result is that the heaviest users pay the lowest average water price. Many cities still using average cost pricing have inverted this rate structure so that they now charge more for each successive block—a sensible way to discourage profligate water use.

Closely related to water pricing is financing of water supply acquisitions and infrastructural improvements. Cities usually subsidize the development of urban water supplies by adding monies from the public coffers to water revenues.

Figure 10: Equilibrium Prices And Quantities With Average Cost And Marginal Cost Pricing Rules

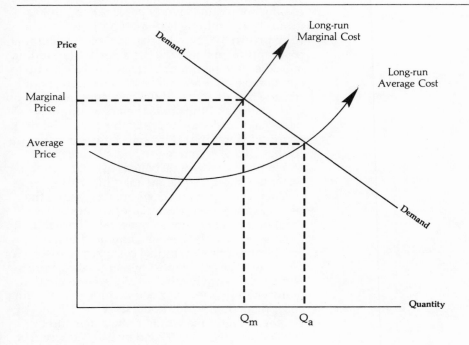

Source: H.J. Vaux, Jr., "Growth and Water in the South Coast Basin of California," draft paper for the World Resources Institute (April 1986) p. 63a

Back-door financing schemes that rely on general city taxes or special bonds in addition to water rate revenues keep water bills artificially low and thus encourage water consumption. Low water prices in western cities may already have aided population expansion beyond what might have occurred with water prices that reflected real costs, and this expansion increases pressures on existing water supplies.

Of course, water pricing policy is linked to social concerns. Policy analysts, citizens, and politicians all want to know how an increase in water rates affects the poor and those on fixed incomes. Also troubling is the inevitable clash with public utility law, which enjoins public water service agencies from profit-making. These two problems are related, and both can be avoided if either a rebate scheme or a "lifeline block" scheme is instituted. In the rebate program, profits made under marginal cost pricing could be redistributed to those for whom the higher water bills represent a hardship. Under a lifeline block program, some initial, necessary quantity of water for the average household is priced well below cost, while additional blocks are priced above cost. On balance, the expense and red tape of administering rebates makes the lifeline scheme the more appealing approach.

From the standpoint of a region's overall water budget, separating household water use into indoor non-consumptive use and outdoor consumptive use is crucial. In most arid cities, municipal wastewater is treated and used to irrigate public parks and golf courses or is appropriated further downstream by other sectors. In some places, treated municipal effluent is traded for higher-quality water from the agricultural sector. Households' consumptive uses, such as lawn irrigation and evaporative air conditioning, are thus the most important to curtail when supplies tighten. Since these are also the uses most responsive to water price, no water service agency can ignore the demand-management potential of rational pricing.

> **Households' consumptive uses, such as lawn irrigation and evaporative air conditioning, are the most important to curtail when supplies tighten. Since these are also the uses most responsive to water price, no water service agency can ignore the demand-management potential of rational pricing.**

Directly regulating household water use is less effective alone than pricing, but it can be a valuable adjunct. Fortuitously, outdoor uses are also the easiest to regulate directly: imposing alternate-day lawn watering and banning ornamental fountains, for example, are not administrative nightmares. At one time or another during droughts, most cities have resorted to these restrictions.

These potential gains notwithstanding, most managers are uncomfortable with the idea of controlling water demand or playing the role of water police. The mandate of most water service agencies is to develop and supply water to meet anticipated demand, whatever it might be. Typically, decisions on overall urban growth and urban planning are left to the city councils and other officials. But things must change. As they find themselves in much the same position as the electric utilities in the mid-1970s, when the cost of new electric plants became prohibitive and the cost of reducing demand justified conservation investments, water service agencies will have to outgrow their traditional role as water purveyors.

Urban water managers should note the success over the last 10 years of energy conservation and education programs initiated by the electric utilities, institutions that once resisted demand management.[57] Clearly, water service agencies can play comparably vital roles in helping consumers use water wisely. Even those agencies with excess capacity today should be conducting pilot programs now so they can run such programs when they are needed. Programs for encouraging conservation by appealing to the consumers' goodwill usually work best in the atmosphere of public camaraderie and civic responsibility brought on by a drought. But education programs can have a longer-lasting effect. Tucson's "beat the peak" campaign is an example of a media blitz launched by a city to educate and enlist public cooperation in voluntary water conservation.[58] When financial incentives are in place, such as rebates or tax credits for purchasing water-saving appliances or landscaping, results are likely to be impressive. Glendale, Arizona, recently instituted a program of rebates to households for automatic sprinkler controls and retrofitted, water-saving toilets.[59] While economists argue that the size of the financial incentive determines the level of participation in such programs, in most residential electric load-control programs, marketing is the more important factor.[60]

On the whole, it is far easier to make recommendations for broad policy change than to implement these innovative programs. The public is accustomed to cheap water—people view unlimited and inexpensive water almost as a basic right. Clearly, in most western cities, citizen awareness and involvement in the activities of their water service agency need improvement.

Unfortunately, the tradition of average cost pricing and the mandate for water provision (as opposed to demand management) are entrenched. One common argument against raising water prices is that municipal water use is not responsive to price. But volumes of evidence from economic and public policy studies say otherwise. Urban water managers also claim that most people are reluctant to accept the "lowering of lifestyle" they think comes with reduced water use. But why not let households themselves decide whether to pay more for their lush lawns and golf courses or to cut back on their water consumption? Because taxes are higher in the end, residents of cities that

One common argument against raising water prices is that municipal water use is not responsive to price. But volumes of evidence from economic and public policy studies say otherwise.

finance supply-side developments rather than raising water prices end up paying one way or another.

Policies for State Water Management

Urban water utilities certainly need to address water demand management. But as long as water users in other sectors have plenty of water and are using it unproductively, another logical step for an urban water manager trying to make ends meet is to try to obtain these local supplies through purchase, lease, or the exercise of eminent domain.

Without question, western agricultural interests feel the pressure to release water supplies for urban uses. Increases in irrigation efficiency could release water for other sectors without significantly decreasing agricultural output or accelerating land retirement. For example, if 90 percent of a state's water consumption is for irrigation, increasing efficiency by just 10 percent would double the amount of water available for urban residences and businesses.

Unfortunately, incentives for water conservation in agriculture are few, and disincentives are ubiquitous. Neither water pricing nor visible opportunity costs encourage the farmer to invest in the technology and management expertise needed to conserve water. Without remuneration or hope of later economic gain, a farmer has no reason to make expensive investments in irrigation efficiency.

A few states have recognized the need to provide conservation incentives. The groundwater mining problem on the Texas High Plains has spurred politicians and agricultural extension officials to ask the state to help the agricultural community by providing low-interest loans, education programs, and subsidies for investment in irrigation technology.[61] But Texas' situation is unique since no other economic sectors are vying for agricultural water supplies, and the local indirect effects of aquifer depletion justify state intervention. In regions with diversified economies, state actions alone cannot expect to offset the lack of economic incentives that would foster broad-scale conservation.

One of the most obvious disincentives to conservation, the low cost of water in agriculture, needs to be redressed. The U.S. Congress and the

> **If 90 percent of a state's water consumption is for irrigation, increasing efficiency by just 10 percent would double the amount of water available for urban residencies and businesses.**

> **One of the most obvious disincentives to conservation, the low cost of water in agriculture, needs to be redressed.**

Bureau of Reclamation traditionally have offered huge subsidies to agriculture. Farmers pay nowhere near the full costs of the federal water they use to irrigate crops, many of which have low water values. Congress struck at this problem when it passed the Reclamation Reform Act of 1982. Among other things, this Act increases from 160 to 960 acres the limit set in 1902 on acreage receiving federally subsidized water. But the subsequent Rules and Regulations require individuals and districts wishing to take advantage of this new limit of 960 acres to amend their contracts with the Bureau of Reclamation and agree to pay full operation and maintenance (O&M) costs on all water received. Beginning in April 1987, irrigation districts that do not amend their contracts must pay the full cost for all water delivered to farmers with more than 160 acres, including interest on unpaid capital plus O&M costs. In the case of the San Luis District in California, the current water price of $10.90 per acre-foot would rise fivefold to $49.89 per acre-foot.[62]

Thus far, the Bureau of Reclamation has been reluctant to implement the pricing provisions of the Act, proposing to collect only the higher O&M costs instead of adding them to current repayment charges. Obviously, the political resistance to lowering subsidies in existing projects makes this a delicate subject. But the Bureau should find ways to renegotiate contracts and reduce federal subsidies to irrigators. And the Congress should certainly require full-cost pricing in any new water projects.

The second disincentive to conserving water in irrigation, the lack of opportunity costs, is also difficult to remedy. Theoretically, a free market for water would produce the necessary price signals and incentives for conservation. If a farmer stood to gain more from selling or leasing his water than from irrigating crops, that water would move from farming to another use of higher value. The operation of a water market could provide the mobility and price signals needed to channel water supplies to the most valuable uses and to maximize total benefits.

A complete change to a water market system with absolute property rights could cause problems in some western states with unappropriated water. The governing philosophy behind the prior appropriation doctrine is that

The Bureau should find ways to renegotiate contracts and reduce federal subsidies to irrigators. And the Congress should certainly require full-cost pricing in any new water projects.

The operation of a water market could provide the mobility and price signals needed to channel water supplies to the most valuable uses and to maximize total benefits.

water belongs to all the people, with the ownership vested in the state as trustee. It would be anathema to the intent of the law to allow people to file for water rights that they intend to sell at a profit rather than use. In those few states with unappropriated supplies, the solution would be to let the states claim any remaining water and manage it for instream flow, or resell it later when other users need the water.

Much more serious challenges to the efficiency of water markets are traditional market failures. With full markets, the general danger is that such public goods as clean water or instream flows for recreation will be under-supplied and that common property resources, such as groundwater aquifers, will be over-utilized. Water-quality protection and preservation of streams and rivers for recreation and wildlife habitat are functions that could fall between the cracks in a competitive marketplace for water, just as they quite explicitly got lost in the past under the prior appropriation doctrine. Expanded water markets could also lead to an increase in groundwater extraction in some areas, as people rush to make profits on their surface rights and resort to pumping groundwater for their own use. A good conjunctive use program, in which surface supplies and groundwater are co-managed, could curb excess extraction.

Despite these potential problems, closing the door on water markets as a way to improve resource management would be a mistake. Western states should clarify property rights in water and emphasize and adjust provisions in prior appropriation law, thus eradicating the obvious barriers to making water resources more flexible and productive. Limited water markets for trading or leasing would provide needed experience and standards for future operations. At the same time, states could help correct the classic market failures: not by replacing market forces with administrative decisions, but by refining the rules and institutions to allow market forces to operate efficiently.

Legal and institutional barriers to water conservation and water markets are numerous.

Unfortunately, legal and institutional barriers to water conservation and water markets are numerous. State laws generally do not give irrigators the property rights to conserved or salvaged water. If a farmer increased irrigation efficiency, the quantity of water saved could not be sold or applied to new lands. Instead, it would remain in the ditch or stream for use by the next senior appropriator. However, California has recently passed a law allowing the sale of conserved and salvaged water. Idaho is also quite liberal in letting irrigators benefit from their conservation efforts. In 1980, its supreme court ruled that an appropriator retains his right for all water, including that salvaged by reducing seepage from transmission systems.[63] On the other hand, Nevada, Arizona, and Wyoming still have counter-productive land appurtenancy requirements that prevent irrigators from using conserved water on other land.

The definition of property rights in water can also hinder water markets through the cost of transfers. In Colorado's adversarial and cumbersome system of water courts, where rights are defined by withdrawal quantities, it is up to the party wishing to sell water to prove that the amount for sale comes from his traditional consumptive use and will not affect return flows. Legal fees and time-consuming proceedings thus remove much of the incentive to transfer water. Changing the basis of a water right from withdrawal quantity for a specified use to consumptive quantity has also been proposed as a way around the high costs of proving consumptive use for each intended transfer.

Another barrier to trade in water is the institutional structure for water use in agriculture.[64] The irrigation district's power lies in its prerogative to approve or veto most transfers: the property rights to water do not reside with the individual irrigator. Obviously, the district management's objectives may not coincide with those of the individual members: the voting system used to elect district supervisors (one vote per acre or property owner, or per dollar of assessed valuation) can skew political power within the district and affect, though not always negatively, its willingness to approve transfers. Nonetheless, western states should keep in mind that these special districts are creatures of the state legislatures, and as such, can be made subject to state water policies.

Some Bureau of Reclamation policies regarding sale of water rights or change in type of use may be additional impediments.[65] Experience in California indicates that water from a project whose original charter included multiple uses may be transferred from agricultural to urban users.

(Transfers among irrigators are allowed in any case.) In projects whose original charter excludes multiple uses, the Bureau policy is not clear-cut, though voluntary exchange of water has been allowed in the past: in the Emery County Project (agriculture only), Utah Power and Light Company was allowed to lease 6,000 acre-feet per year of irrigation water for 40 years.[66] Even though current policies preclude municipal and industrial users from enjoying the entire subsidy, Bureau contractors can nonetheless realize large profits on water sold.

Not surprisingly, many taxpayers disapprove of the potential windfall created if irrigation districts are allowed to receive federally-subsidized water and then to turn around and sell that water at market prices. But the resulting increases in irrigation efficiency, with concomitant decreases in salinity and other water quality problems, lower the taxpayers' water cleanup bills. And the overall gain in efficiency within the particular basin can offset the windfall further: urban dwellers are better off buying some agricultural water than developing new, expensive supply projects. In fact, both the irrigators, who can sell their water for more than its worth in growing crops, and cities, which can delay or even abandon plans for new projects, win.[67] In the South Coast Basin of California, the gains resulting from trade between the Imperial Irrigation District, the southern agricultural areas, and the cities, could reach $100 million per year by 2000, and almost $150 million per year by 2020, not including the benefits of water quality improvement.[68]

A related problem is the oft-heard argument that expanded water markets could indirectly harm rural communities serving agricultural areas. Yet, because the irrigation water budget is so substantial in every western state, lots of water can be freed up with rather minor efficiency adjustments, changes that should not eliminate agriculture entirely. Where a substantial decline in agricultural activity is foreseen, the erosion of public revenues for such expenditures as schools and roads is a genuine concern.[69]

Fortunately, there is a compromise position on the questions of windfalls and the indirect effects of water sales: some of the windfall can be recaptured by the federal, state, and local governments when water is transferred out of agriculture, and some of the windfall can be

> **Many taxpayers disapprove of the potential windfall created if irrigation districts are allowed to receive federally-subsidized water and then to turn around and sell that water at market prices... But both the irrigators, who can sell their water for more than its worth in growing crops, and cities, which can delay or even abandon plans for new projects, win.**

reaped by the farmer. In implementing such a proposal, the proportion to the farmer should be sufficient to preserve the incentive to sell, the federal government should get some repayment for the national tax-payer who initially financed the projects, and the state and local governments should collect enough to ameliorate any adverse local effects of reduced agricultural activity.

Beyond the legal and political barriers to water markets, states need to consider the vehicles for water trading. Ideally, water rights could be sold or rented. Because leasing preserves the ownership of the right, it appeals to speculators and those who want a water hedge for times of drought. Conditional leasing is another attractive alternative, especially to cities that may need extra supplies only during droughts. One particularly flexible, but nonetheless formal, mechanism for handling trades is water banking. This approach allows a user with excess water to voluntarily "deposit" part or all of that water in return for a market-determined price. Deposits may be temporary, annual, or long-term, and they can be withdrawn by other users for a fee. Of course, water banking is limited in scope by the water-delivery system's physical constraints, and it requires extensive data collection and bookkeeping. But it has worked before. During the 1976–1977 drought, the state of California and the Bureau of Reclamation arranged for water owned by the Metropolitan Water District but stored in the San Joaquin Valley to be sold to farmers in the Valley and, through exchange agreements, to municipal water users in northern California.[70] State water laws will not have to be revised completely to allow other such water banks to operate since water banking can be designated a beneficial use, thus allaying irrigators' fears of losing their water rights through nonuse.

Besides eliminating the barriers to effective water markets, state governments have a distinct role in redressing the inefficiencies that result when the private and social benefits and costs of water use diverge significantly. Nowhere is this role more important than in instream flow and water quality protection.

Most western states have laws that recognize instream flow rights. But until the states systematically investigate their instream flow needs and exercise their legal authority to protect

Until the states systematically investigate their instream flow needs and exercise their legal authority to protect minimum flows, disputes over instream flows will chill the transfer of water rights.

minimum flows, disputes over instream flows chill the transfer of water rights. Ideally, state agencies, in close cooperation with federal land management agencies and Indian tribes, should investigate every river reach, decide on the appropriate level of flow, and provide legal protection. This protection could include appropriating water under the name of state or federal rights, setting minimum streamflows beyond which water cannot be removed offstream, defining instream flow as a beneficial use open to individual or group appropriation, or legislating protection directly through a state-level wild or scenic rivers act. In addition, the Public Trust Doctrine, extended to inland rivers as it has been in California and Idaho, could prove a valuable legal aid to groups fighting reduced streamflows and other environmental impacts of out-of-basin water transfers.[71]

Besides protecting instream flow quantities, states should protect instream flow quality. But progress in salinity control has been disappointing. The delay in implementing effective control measures does not reflect a lack of technically feasible or cost-effective measures: on-farm management practices that reduce leaching, deep percolation, and saline surface runoff are the most economical way to lessen the salt load from irrigation. Rather, effective basinwide policies are few primarily because those most responsible for the problem see nothing to gain from reducing their saline outflows or, in the extreme case, retiring their lands. Thus, the focus has been on measures whose costs can be shared broadly even if they are not the most cost-effective means of control. For example, the projected capital cost for implementing the Bureau's water quality improvement package in Grand Valley, Colorado, is $280 million (in 1984 dollars), a sum that will be met entirely with federal funds.[72] The primary beneficiaries—to the tune of $15 million a year— are not the Grand Valley irrigators, but downstream water users in Arizona and southern California.

Traditionally, the Bureau of Reclamation's salinity control programs have been such capital-intensive, structural projects as diverting river flows around natural sources of salinity, building desalination plants, or lining water-delivery canals with concrete—invariably expensive undertakings. Given continued cost escalations, shrinking

Progress in salinity control has been disappointing. The delay in implementing effective control measures does not reflect a lack of technically feasible or cost-effective measures: on-farm management practices that reduce leaching, deep percolation, and saline surface runoff are the most economical way to lessen the salt load from irrigation.

The new emphasis of
state and Bureau
programs should be
on controlling salinity
from irrigated
agriculture.

federal budgets for water projects, and the demonstrated economies of on-farm measures, salinity control in the Colorado River Basin and elsewhere must change. First, states need to monitor and track salinity levels so that the sub-basins contributing the most salt can be held accountable and progress in water quality can be measured. Second, the new emphasis of state and Bureau programs should be on controlling salinity from irrigated agriculture—reducing deep percolation, minimizing salt leaching, changing to crops needing less water, and retiring highly saline and marginally productive lands. In short, water use should be made much more efficient. And the ideal encouragement would come from higher water prices and active water markets. Combined with numerical standards, direct regulation, and damage assessment by the states, water markets would provide the necessary incentives to irrigators to improve their efficiency and lower their saline seepage and runoff.

Just like salinity, toxic elements in agricultural return flows pose extensive environmental problems. The pollution of Kesterson Wildlife Refuge in California's Central Valley is the most celebrated example of selenium's fatal consequences for fish and wildlife, though the problem is widespread.[73] Also like salinity-cleanup programs, selenium cleanup can be phenomenally expensive once the element has concentrated to lethal proportions in marshes and lakes. Once again, who pays? The taxpayer is not likely to subsidize ongoing cleanup and disposal programs for the toxic by-product of an already heavily subsidized irrigation operation. As with salinity, the optimal solution is to encourage farmers with drainage problems to sell their water at market prices and retire their lands from production.

Policies for Interstate Water Management

The prior appropriation doctrine that governs water rights within states colors the way water is viewed among states. As noted, the Colorado River Compact assigns shares of Colorado River flows to the basin states, with the stipulation that if an Upper Basin state cannot utilize its entire share, the excess water flows downstream to satisfy water demands in the Lower Basin states. While this division does ensure that the Upper

Basin holds paper rights to develop its water, it also impedes efficient basin-wide water use. So long as an Upper Basin state cannot benefit from unused releases to the Lower Basin and fears the loss of its water rights in the future, it will continue to support uneconomic water development projects and inefficient water use within its borders. The Central Utah Project and the Dolores and Animas-La Plata projects in Colorado exemplify this pre-emptive development: Utah and Colorado citizens want to know for certain that Colorado River supplies will be there when they need them, whether for agricultural or municipal use.[74]

In a sense, under Colorado River Compact provisions, the states do not even own their waters. Colorado cannot charge Los Angeles for the unused outflows that eventually provide that city with part of its municipal water supply. However, the Lower Basin users could collectively pay the Upper Basin states not to further divert and develop their entitlements if such interstate water agreements and water markets were allowed. The problem with a specific irrigation district, for instance, entering into negotiations with a Lower Basin city to sell unused water is that those released waters, legally, should go automatically to the next senior appropriator. The Colorado River flows that reach California are allocated on a strict priority basis, with large irrigation districts—not cities—at the top of the list. The Galloway Group's plan to sell surface water from Colorado to municipal users in San Diego is a case in point.[75] To date, no compact explicitly allows water sales across state lines. Some legal experts suggest that interstate transactions with water that has been ''property-ized,'' or allocated by the prior appropriation system within an Upper Basin state, will be possible under certain interpretations of Compact provisions. But difficult questions surround water that has not been given a vested property right thus far by an Upper Basin state.[76]

The dilemma surrounding management of the Colorado River is that the Upper Basin states continue to use water inefficiently and to invest in uneconomic projects despite the sizable economic values of water (both instream and offstream) derived from letting water flow downstream to the Lower Basin instead. The crux of the matter is that the Upper Basin states cannot share in those returns. Additionally, while the Bureau of Reclamation, the U.S. Environmental Protection Agency, and the states continue to search for cost-effective solutions, salinity continues to be the major water quality problem in the Colorado River, with the Upper Basin states contributing most of the salt load and the Lower Basin states shouldering the costs of lowered water quality.

Today's emerging conflicts in the Colorado River Basin highlight problems that will only worsen if current policies are continued. The states of the Colorado River Compact now need to reorder their water development priorities, facilitate fair and equitable interstate water markets, and improve the current fragmented and inefficient management of a valuable and scarce resource. This tall order will require a great deal of cooperation and discussion among the states—they need to devise a forum for resolving disputes and anticipating and heading off new problems—and will be furthered if the states get serious about data gathering, water quality monitoring, and developing appropriate compensatory arrangements. Clearly, western states must act in concert. Unless the rules and customs of the Colorado River can be adjusted to the changing demands being placed upon it, intrusion by the federal government, the courts, and the Congress will escalate.

In addition to resolving some of the externalities of salinity and instream flow benefits, interpretation and evolution of the Colorado River Compact and state agreements to include interstate water markets could help alleviate some of the dilemmas faced by rapidly growing western cities. As noted, many of the urban areas in the arid reaches of the Southwest, such as Tucson, are facing stark limitations on their water supplies. But because the physical components of the delivery system are in place—the River itself and the various aqueducts that carry water to central Arizona and Southern California—water markets could enable cities in the Lower Basin to keep up with their growing water demands. Despite this optimism, however, these cities must remember that reallocating irrigation water through an interstate water market, helpful as it may be in the short term, cannot solve all the problems of unchecked urban growth.

> **Unless the rules and customs of the Colorado River can be adjusted to the changing demands being placed upon it, intrusion by the federal government, the courts, and the Congress will escalate.**

VIII. Summary and Conclusions

The arid American West has entered a new era. What was once the endless frontier is now a vital, populated region fully integrated with the rest of the country. What were once seemingly endless stores of natural wealth—water, land, forests, blue skies—are now resources under stress. Water, one of the West's most vital resources, is no less physically abundant today than it was decades ago, but it is now oversubscribed and, often, polluted.

Water is no less physically abundant today than it was decades ago, but it is now oversubscribed and, often polluted.

In light of emerging conflicts over water allocation and water quality degradation, western states must now re-evaluate their water management priorities. Because of recent increases in water demand for cities and for recreation and instream flow protection, water supplies are being stretched to their limits. The laws and institutions governing natural resources in the old West have survived the transition from plenty to scarcity, but may not be providing the best, most efficient resource management under today's conditions of rapid population growth and urbanization. Although irrigation remains by far the largest western water user, urban thirst threatens traditional water-use patterns.

Growing urban demand is not the only threat to agricultural water use, either: soil and water salinity and toxic return flows highlight the negative environmental impacts of traditional irrigation practices. The usual structural strategies for addressing water quality problems, such as cleaning up rivers downstream from the saline sources, are phenomenally expensive and economically unwarranted when compared to cheaper, on-farm alternatives. But just as water quantity problems are not easily solved with existing rules and customs for water allocation, neither are water quality problems.

The time-honored strategy of increasing water supplies and correcting water quality degradation through capital-intensive projects has reached its limits: financial, environmental, and legal obstacles are overwhelming. Yet, improving water's productivity and mobility could enable the states not merely to survive, but to thrive in this era of water shortages. For the most part, non-structural water management should replace structural water development. At the heart of decisions on water resources management should be a "least-cost" accounting—incorporating all the environmental and third party costs of any proposed path.

> For the most part, non-structural water management should replace structural water development. At the heart of decisions on water resources management should be a "least-cost" accounting—incorporating all the environmental and third party costs of any proposed path.

Policies for Urban Water Service Agencies

Cities should price water at its marginal cost, allowing individuals to decide whether to reduce their consumption or to pay the real cost of their additional water usage. A rate structure consisting of a lifeline block with increasing block rates (for increasing use) would induce consumers to conserve water, while protecting the poor from financial hardship. Higher summer rates could also help reduce the outdoor, consumptive portion of household water use and shave peak water demand. Education and technical assistance programs designed to enlighten consumers about rate structures and water-efficient landscaping would be necessary and valuable adjuncts to marginal cost pricing.

Growing cities that have already instituted marginal cost pricing and are still seeking to expand their water supplies should follow least-cost rules in choosing between new water supply projects and such alternatives as purchase or lease of water from agriculture (including irrigation efficiency investments in exchange for water supplies), or investment in demand-reduction programs. In many cases, water service agencies may discover that "new" supplies found through water conservation programs are cheaper than new supplies obtained through system expansion, or even through the purchase of irrigation water rights.

Even full mobility of water supplies and much more efficient water use cannot change the fact that much of the West is a desert, or close to it.

Finally, even full mobility of water supplies and much more efficient water use cannot change the fact that much of the West is a desert, or close to it. The wild places and open spaces of the West will not thrive along current paths of maximum urban growth and development.

State Water Management

Western states should remove constraints to efficient water use and effective water markets. Active water markets could provide users, especially irrigators, with the opportunity costs needed to spur efficiency improvements and sales of excess water to other users. Depending on the state, the barriers to trade in water consist of outdated water rights definitions, transaction costs, entrenched customs, and restrictive clauses in state water laws and interstate compacts. States should legislate, or merely institute through their agencies, many of the needed policies. They could legalize the resale of conserved or salvaged water, facilitate water banking, designate conditional leasing as a "beneficial" use, or direct irrigation districts to allow state project water sales to other users.

Barriers to water markets also reside in Bureau of Reclamation policies that tie federal water supplies to agricultural uses on certain lands. The Bureau should amend and clarify its rules to allow sales and leases of federal water to non-agricultural users outside the irrigation district's boundaries.

As a natural response to water markets, higher water-use efficiency in irrigated agriculture would free more water for present and future uses, and would also have many positive environmental consequences—saline and toxic return flows from irrigation would be reduced, and supplies would be available to augment flows for recreation or waste dilution. Everyone would be made better off: cities could buy water cheaper than they could build new projects, national tax-payers would not be asked to foot ever-higher salinity-control and water-development bills, and farmers could sell water for more than its return in irrigated crop production.

While states remove constraints to water markets, they also need to protect water uses that fall outside the usual market allocations. Minimum instream flows needed for fish and wildlife habitat, recreation, and waste dilution must be investigated, allocated, and protected physically as well as legally. Potential policies include state or private appropriation, minimum streamflow regulation, or legislated protection. In addition to the amount of water in streams, protecting the water's quality is also the responsibility of the state and federal governments. Effective salinity control can be achieved through on-farm irrigation management programs and active water markets—both leading to increased irrigation efficiency and the retirement of marginal lands. Accountability among sub-basins is an essential prerequisite to any successful salinity control program.

Interstate Water Management

The institutional management of the Colorado River was initiated to make sure that prior appropriation of the Colorado River by the faster-growing Lower Basin states did not stymie development in the Upper Basin states. Today, this goal is being accomplished, but at tremendous cost to the basin-wide efficiency of water use. The benefits from the river's use are not being equitably shared or maximized under the current system, in which the Upper Basin is compelled to develop water resources pre-emptively and pays no price for its heavy contribution to downstream salinity.

Considering these pervasive inefficiencies and the overall increases in water demand throughout the Basin, states need to work together to divide the costs and benefits of Colorado River use more efficiently and equitably. Interstate water markets and leasing arrangements should be encouraged and fostered.

* * * *

These policies for western cities and states are rooted in the common-sense notions that water supplies are limited, that the arid and semi-arid regions are going to have to live within their water budgets, and that raising the productivity, substitutability, and mobility of water will ease the overall conditions of economic scarcity. In short, western water needs to work harder.

Western water needs to work harder.

These recommendations also stem from the realization that many of the traditional water policies set in place when the West had fewer people and a simpler economy no longer serve the public interest and need to be adjusted to new challenges, including urbanization and environmental degradation. Resolving emerging conflicts over water will require creative and sometimes controversial steps—but the West should act now, *before* crises govern the management of this vital resource.

Dr. Mohamed T. El-Ashry is a Senior Associate and Director of WRI's Arid Lands Project. **Diana C. Gibbons** is an independent consultant.

APPENDIX A

Case Studies and Authors

AGRICULTURAL CASE STUDIES

Upper Colorado River Basin
Charles Howe and W. Ashley Ahrens
University of Colorado, Boulder

Central Valley, California
Charles Moore and Richard Howitt
University of California at Davis

High Plains, Texas
Ronald Lacewell and John Lee
Texas A&M University

URBAN CASE STUDIES

Denver
Gordon Milliken
Denver Research Institute

Tucson
William Martin, Helen Ingram, Dennis Cory,
and Mary Wallace
University of Arizona, Tucson

Southern California
Henry Vaux, Jr.
University of California at Riverside

APPENDIX B

WORLD RESOURCES INSTITUTE

Workshop on Water and the Arid Lands of the West

February 20–21, 1986
Ramada Inn—Downtown
Tucson, Arizona

Participants

Thomas G. Bahr	Director, Water Resources Research Institute, New Mexico State University, Las Cruces, New Mexico (former Director, Office of Water Policy, U.S. Department of Interior)
Clifford I. Barrett	Regional Director, U.S. Bureau of Reclamation, Salt Lake City, Utah
D. Craig Bell	Executive Director, Western States Water Council, Salt Lake City, Utah
Paul Bloom	Attorney, Washington, D.C. (former General Counsel, New Mexico State Engineer's Office)
Frank Brooks	Director, Tucson Water Department, Tucson, Arizona
F. Lee Brown	Professor of Economics and Co-Director, Natural Resources Center, University of New Mexico, Albuquerque, New Mexico
Thomas Burbey	Chief, Operation Division, U.S. Bureau of Reclamation, Phoenix, Arizona
Jerald Butchert	Manager, Westlands Water District, Fresno, California
Jeris Danielson	Colorado State Engineer, Colorado Division of Water Resources, Denver, Colorado
Charlene Dougherty	Director of Legislation, National Audubon Society, Washington, DC
Harold E. Dregne	Director, International Center for Arid Lands Studies, Texas Tech University, Lubbock, Texas
Bruce Driver	Scholar in Residence, Western Governors' Association, Denver, Colorado

Mohamed T. El-Ashry	Senior Associate, World Resources Institute, Washington, DC
Hubert A. Farbes, Jr.	Member, Denver Water Board, Denver, Colorado
John A. Folk-Williams	President, Western Network, Santa Fe, New Mexico
Kenneth E. Foster	Director, Office of Arid Lands Studies, University of Arizona, Tucson, Arizona
Kenneth Frederick	Senior Fellow and Director, Renewable Resources Division, Resources for the Future, Washington, DC
David H. Getches	Executive Director, Department of Natural Resources, Denver, Colorado
Diana C. Gibbons	Consultant, World Resources Institute, Washington, DC
Roy M. Gray	Special Assistant for Legislative Affairs, U.S. Department of Agriculture, Washington, DC
Frank Gregg	Director, School of Renewable Natural Resources, University of Arizona, Tucson, Arizona (former Director, U.S. Bureau of Land Management)
Robert M. Hagan	Professor, Department of Land, Air and Water Resources, University of California, Davis, California
Charles Howe	Professor, Department of Economics, University of Colorado, Boulder, Colorado
Richard Howitt	Professor, Department of Agricultural Economics, University of California, Davis, California
Helen Ingram	Professor, Political Science Department, University of Arizona, Tucson, Arizona
R. Craig Kennedy	Vice President, Program and Planning, The Joyce Foundation, Chicago, Illinois
Robert King	Director, Office of Natural Resources, Texas Department of Agriculture, Austin, Texas
H.O. Kunkel	Dean, College of Agriculture, Texas A&M University, College Station, Texas
Ronald Lacewell	Professor, Agricultural Economics Department, Texas A&M University, College Station, Texas

79

John Leshy	Professor of Law, Arizona State University, College of Law, Tempe, Arizona (former Assistant Solicitor, U.S. Department of Interior)
William B. Lord	Director, Arizona Water Resource Research Center, University of Arizona, Tucson, Arizona
Daniel Luecke	Staff Scientist, Environmental Defense Fund, Boulder, Colorado
Lawrence J. MacDonnell	Director, Natural Resources Law Center, University of Colorado, School of Law, Boulder, Colorado
Dean E. Mann	Professor, Department of Political Science, University of California, Santa Barbara, California
William E. Martin	Professor, Department of Agricultural Economics, University of Arizona, Tucson, Arizona
Don Maughan	Engineering Consultant, Carmichael, California (former Deputy Director, Water Management, State of Arizona; former Chairman of the California State Water Resources Control Board)
Murray J. McGregor	Professor, Farm Management Department, Lincoln College, Canterbury, New Zealand
Charles Meyers	Attorney, Gibson, Dunn, and Crutcher, Denver, Colorado (former Dean, Stanford Law School)
William H. Miller	Manager, Denver Water Department, Denver, Colorado
Gordon Milliken	Senior Research Economist, Denver Research Institute, University of Denver, Denver, Colorado
Charles Moore	Professor, Department of Agricultural Economics, University of California, Davis, California
Christine Olsenius	Vice President, Freshwater Foundation, Navarre, Minnesota
George Pring	Professor of Law, University of Denver, College of Law, Denver, Colorado
James J. Riley	Consultant, Environmental Research Laboratory, Tucson, Arizona
Priscilla Robinson	Executive Director, Southwest Environmental Services, Tucson, Arizona

Ralph Roming	Commissioner, Texas Water Commission, Austin, Texas
Paul Singer	Chief of Operations, Metropolitan Water District, Los Angeles, California
Gus Speth	President, World Resources Institute, Washington, DC
Henry Vaux, Jr.	Professor, Department of Soil and Environmental Sciences, University of California, Riverside, California
Gary Weatherford	President, Watershed West, Berkeley, California
John G. Welles	Regional Administrator, U.S. Environmental Protection Agency, Region VIII, Denver, Colorado
Richard M. Welles	Deputy Director, Arizona State Water Resources Department, Phoenix, Arizona
Zach Willey	Senior Economist, Environmental Defense Fund, Berkeley, California

APPENDIX C

Advisory Panel

Arid Lands Project

Paul Bloom

Attorney; former General Counsel, New Mexico State Water Engineer's Office

John Bryson

Senior Vice President, Southern California Edison Company

Harold E. Dregne

Director, International Center for Arid and Semi-Arid Lands Studies, Texas Tech University

Robert M. Hagan

Professor, Department of Land, Air and Water Resources, University of California at Davis

Jim Hightower

Commissioner of Agriculture, State of Texas

Carl N. Hodges

Director, Environmental Research Laboratory, University of Arizona

Helen Ingram

Professor of Political Science, University of Arizona

H. O. Kunkel

Dean, College of Agriculture, Texas A&M University

Dean E. Mann

Professor of Political Science, University of California at Santa Barbara

Don Maughan

Deputy Director, Water Management, State of Arizona (now Chairman of the California State Water Resources Control Board)

Charles Meyers

Gibson, Dunn, and Crutcher, Denver; former Dean, Stanford Law School

Gilbert White

Gustavson Distinguished Professor Emeritus of Geography, Institute of Behavioral Sciences, University of Colorado

Zach Willey

Senior Economist, Environmental Defense Fund, Berkeley

Notes

1. U.S. Geological Survey, *National Water Summary 1983-Hydrologic Events and Issues,* Water Supply Paper no. 2250 (Washington, D.C.: U.S. Government Printing Office, 1984) p. 1.

2. *Ibid,* Table 2.

3. U.S. Department of Commerce, Bureau of the Census, *Statistical Abstract of the United States-1981* (Washington, D.C.: Government Printing Office, December 1981) "USA Statistics in Brief" (supplement) and Table 23.

4. Council on Environmental Quality, *Environmental Quality-1980* (Washington, D.C.: U.S. Government Printing Office, December 1980) p. 346.

5. James A. Ruffner and Frank E. Bair, *The Weather Almanac,* 3rd Edition (Detroit, Michigan: Gale Research Company, 1981).

6. This section on the development of western water law based on Norris Hundley, Jr., *Water and the West* (Berkeley: University of California Press, 1975), and Terry L. Anderson, *Water Crisis: Ending the Policy Drought* (Baltimore: Johns Hopkins University Press, 1983) Chapter III.

7. George W. Pring and Karen A. Tomb, "License to Waste: Legal Barriers to Conservation and Efficient Use of Water in the West," *Proceedings of the Twenty-fifth Annual Rocky Mountain Mineral Law Institute,* vol. 25, no. 1 (1979) pp. 25–67.

8. Gary D. Weatherford and Gordon C. Jacoby, "Impact of Energy Development on the Law of the Colorado River," *Natural Resources Journal,* vol. 15, no. 1 (1975) pp. 171–213.

9. John D. Leshy, "Special Water Districts—The Historical Background," in James N. Corbridge, Jr., ed., *Special Water Districts: Challenge for the Future*, Proceedings of the Workshop on Special Water Districts held at the University of Colorado, September 12–13, 1983 (Boulder, Colorado: University of Colorado School of Law, 1983) pp. 11–30.

10. E. Phillip LeVeen and Laura B. King, *Turning Off the Tap on Federal Water Subsidies* (San Francisco: Natural Resources Defense Council and the California Rural Legal Assistance Foundation, August 1985) vol. 1, p. 3.

11. U.S. Department of Commerce, *Statistical Abstract-1981*, "USA Statistics in Brief" (supplement).

12. U.S. Council on Environmental Quality, *Environmental Quality-1980*, p. 347.

13. U.S. Department of Commerce, *Statistical Abstract-1981*, "USA Statistics in Brief" (supplement).

14. John D. Leshy, "Unveiling the Sagebrush Rebellion: Law, Politics, and Federal Lands," *U.C. Davis Law Review*, vol. 14, no. 2 (Winter 1980) p. 347.

15. U.S. Geological Survey, *National Water Summary 1983*.

16. *Ibid.*

17. Kenneth D. Frederick and James C. Hanson, *Water for Western Agriculture* (Washington, D.C.: Resources for the Future, 1984) p. 1.

18. Frederick and Hanson, *Water for Western Agriculture*, p. 241.

19. U.S. Bureau of Reclamation, *Summary Statistics* (Washington, D.C.: 1984) vol. 1, "Water, Land, and Related Data," p. 6.

20. B. Delworth Gardner, "Water Pricing and Rent Seeking in California Agriculture," in Terry L. Anderson, ed., *Water Rights: Scarce Resource Allocation, Bureaucracy, and the Environment* (Cambridge, Massachusetts: Ballinger, 1983) pp. 83–113.

21. Ronald D. Lacewell and John G. Lee, "Land and Water Management Issues: Texas High Plains," a paper prepared for a forthcoming World Resources Institute book, to be published by Cambridge University Press.

22. Frederick and Hanson, *Water for Western Agriculture*, p. 25.

23. Diana C. Gibbons, *The Economic Value of Water* (Washington, D.C.: Resources for the Future, 1986) p. 33.

24. Mohamed T. El-Ashry, Jan van Schilfgaarde, and Susan Schiffman, "Salinity Pollution from Irrigated Agriculture," *Journal of Soil and Water Conservation*, vol. 40, no. 1 (January–February 1985) pp. 48–52.

25. Mohamed T. El-Ashry, "Salinity Problems Related to Irrigated Agriculture in Arid Regions," *Proceedings of Third Conference on Egypt and the Year 2000* (Cairo: Association of Egyptian-American Scholars, 1978) pp. 55–74.

26. U.S. Bureau of Reclamation, *Colorado River Water Quality Improvement Program* (Denver: U.S. Bureau of Reclamation, 1983).

27. U.S. Environmental Protection Agency, *The Mineral Quality Problem in the Colorado River Basin* (Washington, D.C.: Government Printing Office, 1971).

28. Mohamed T. El-Ashry, "Groundwater Salinity Problems Related to Irrigation in the Colorado River Basin," *Ground Water*, vol. 18, no. 1 (January–February 1980) pp. 37–45.

29. D.J. Dudek and G.L. Horner, "Integrated Physical-Economic Resource Analysis: A Case Study of the San Joaquin Valley," (Ada, Oklahoma: Robert S. Kerr Environmental Laboratory, U.S. Environmental Protection Agency, 1981).

30. John D. Hedlund, "USDA Planning Process for Colorado River Basin Salinity Control," in Richard H. French, ed., *Salinity in Watercourses and Reservoirs*, (Stoneham, Massachusetts: Butterworth Publishing Co., 1984) pp. 63–77.

31. U.S. Environmental Protection Agency, *Evaluation of Salinity Created by Irrigation Return Flows* (Washington, D.C.: 1974) p. 36.

32. U.S. Bureau of Reclamation, *Colorado River Water Quality Improvement Program*.

33. A.P. Kleinman and F.B. Brown, "Colorado River Salinity: Economic Impacts on Agricultural, Municipal and Industrial Users," (Denver: U.S. Bureau of Reclamation, 1980) p. 19.

34. U.S. Bureau of Reclamation, California Department of Water Resources, and California State Water Resources Control Board, *Agricultural Drainage and Salt Management in the San Joaquin Valley* (Fresno: San Joaquin Valley Interagency Drainage Program, 1979).

35. Data and information in this section from Charles V. Moore and Richard Howitt, ''The Central Valley of California,'' a paper prepared for a forthcoming World Resources Institute book, to be published by Cambridge University Press.

36. ''Water Districts File Suit to Block Rate Hikes,'' Chico, California *Enterprise Record*, June 28, 1986.

37. Data and information in this section from Lacewell and Lee, ''Land and Water Management Issues: Texas High Plains.''

38. ''Conservation Plan Falls Short of Goals,'' *Washington Post*, June 10, 1986.

39. Data and information in this section from Charles W. Howe and W. Ashley Ahrens, ''The Land and Water Resources of the Upper Colorado River Basin: Problems and Policy Alternatives,'' a paper prepared for a forthcoming World Resources Institute book, to be published by Cambridge University Press.

40. This discussion of municipal water demand based on Diana C. Gibbons, *The Economic Value of Water*, pp. 7–21.

41. U.S. Geological Survey, *National Water Summary 1983*. It is important to note that this figure is not quality adjusted: compared to agricultural runoff, municipal effluent may be a higher percentage of withdrawal but may be virtually useless for other uses until it undergoes expensive treatment.

42. For example, the figure is 61 percent for Arizona, 41 percent for California, and 6 percent for New Hampshire. These figures calculated from data in U.S. Geological Survey, *National Water Summary 1983*.

43. David H. Getches, ''Meeting Colorado's Water Requirements: An Overview of the Issues,'' paper presented at the conference, ''Colorado Water Issues and Options: the 90's and Beyond,'' Natural Resources Law Center, University of Colorado School of Law (October 8–9, 1985) p. 11.

44. Diana C. Gibbons, *The Economic Value of Water*, p. 18.

45. For example, see Charles W. Howe and F.P. Linaweaver, Jr., "The Impact of Price on Residential Water Demand and Its Relation to System Design and Price Structure,": *Water Resources Research,* vol. 3, no. 1 (First Quarter 1967) pp. 13–32; Leon E. Danielson, "Estimation of Residential Water Demand," Economics Research Report no. 39 (Raleigh: North Carolina State University, October 1977); Angelo P. Grima, *Residential Water Demand: Alternative Choices for Management* (Toronto, Ontario: University of Toronto Press, 1972); and Henry S. Foster, Jr. and Bruce R. Beattie, "Urban Residential Demand for Water in the United States," *Land Economics,* vol. 55, no. 1 (February 1979) pp. 43–58.

46. Getches, "Meeting Colorado's Water Requirements," p. 29.

47. John A. Folks-Williams, Susan C. Fry and Lucy Hilgendorf, *Western Water Flows to the Cities,* vol. 3 of *Water in the West* (Santa Fe, New Mexico: Western Network; and Corelo, California: Island Press, 1985).

48. Data and information in this section from Henry J. Vaux, "Growth and Water in the South Coast Basin of California," a paper prepared for a forthcoming World Resources Institute book, to be published by Cambridge University Press.

49. Data and information in this section from William E. Martin, Helen M. Ingram, Dennis C. Cory, and Mary G. Wallace, "Toward Sustaining A Desert Metropolis: Water and Land Use in Tucson, Arizona," a paper prepared for a forthcoming World Resources Institute book, to be published by Cambridge University Press.

50. Data and information in this section from J. Gordon Milliken, "Water Management Issues in the Denver, Colorado Urban Area," a paper prepared for a forthcoming World Resources Institute book, to be published by Cambridge University Press.

51. Gibbons, *The Economic Value of Water.*

52. Cass Peterson, "California's Liquid Asset," *Washington Post,* November 3, 1985.

53. Vaux, "Growth and Water in the South Coast Basin of California."

54. See Terry L. Anderson, ed., *Water Rights: Scarce Resource Allocation, Bureaucracy, and the Environment.*

55. Martin, et al., "Toward Sustaining a Desert Metropolis."

56. Vaux, "Growth and Water in the South Coast Basin of California."

57. *Demand-Side Management: Overview of Key Issues* (Washington, D.C.: Edison Electric Institute and Electric Power Research Institute, 1984).

58. William E. Martin, Helen M. Ingram, Nancy K. Laney, and Adrian H. Griffin, *Saving Water in a Desert City* (Washington, D.C.: Resources for the Future, 1984) pp. 87–88.

59. "U.S. Water News," vol. 2, no. 10 (April 1986).

60. A.G. Lawrence, T.A. Heberlein, and R.M. Baumgartner, *Customer Attitudes and Responses to Load Management,* paper prepared for the Electric Power Research Institute (Palo Alto, California, 1984).

61. Lacewell and Lee, "Land and Water Management Issues."

62. LeVeen and King, *Turning Off the Tap on Federal Subsidies.*

63. Steven J. Shupe, "Wasted Water: the Problems and Promise of Improving Efficiency Under Western Water Law," paper presented at the conference "Colorado Water Issues and Options: the 90's and Beyond," Natural Resources Law Center, University of Colorado School of Law (October 8–9, 1985) p. 20.

64. Dwight R. Lee, "Political Provision of Water: An Economic/Public Choice Perspective," in James N. Corbridge, Jr., ed., *Special Water Districts: Challenge for the Future,* Proceedings of the Workshop on Special Water Districts held at the University of Colorado, September 12–13, 1983 (Boulder, Colorado: University of Colorado School of Law, 1983) pp. 51–70.

65. The Bureau of Reclamation may change its policy to allow transfers out of irrigation. See "Free Market Proposed," *U.S. Water News,* vol. 2, no. 11 (May 1986) p. 1.

66. "Meeting Water Needs through the Voluntary Exchange of Water—Continuation of Past Policy," staff paper (Washington, D.C.: Office of Policy Analysis, U.S. Department of the Interior, 1983) p. 5.

67. Zach Willey, *Economic Development and Environmental Quality in California's Water System* (Institute of

Governmental Studies at the University of
California, Berkeley, 1985).

68. Vaux, "Growth and Water in the South Coast Basin
of California."

69. Ernest A. Engelbert and Ann Foley Scheuring, eds.,
Water Scarcity: Impacts on Western Agriculture
(Berkeley: University of California Press, 1984) part
III.

70. U.S. General Accounting Office, "Better Water
Management and Conservation Possible—But
Constraints Need to be Overcome" (Washington,
D.C.: 1978) p. 22.

71. Steven J. Shupe, "Emerging Forces in Western
Water Law," *Resource Law Notes*, no. 8 (Boulder:
Natural Resources Law Center at the University of
Colorado, April 1986) p. 2.

72. El-Ashry, et al., "Salinity Pollution."

73. Richard W. Wahl, "Cleaning Up Kesterson,"
Resources Newsletter (Washington, D.C.: Resources
for the Future, Spring 1986) p. 11.

74. Testimony of Dr. Mohamed T. El-Ashry before the
Department of the Interior Water Projects Review
Team, Hearings on Fruitland Mesa, Dolores, and
Savery-Pot Hook Water Projects (March 21, 1977).

75. Sharon P. Gross, "The Galloway Project and the
Colorado River Compacts: Will the Compacts Bar
Transbasin Water Diversions?" *Natural Resources
Journal*, vol. 25 (October 1985) pp. 935–960.

76. Charles J. Meyers, personal communication, May
19, 1986.

WRI PUBLICATIONS ORDER FORM

ORDER NO.	TITLE	QTY	TOTAL $
B719	*Bordering on Trouble: Resources and Politics in Latin America* edited by Andrew Maguire and Janet Welsh Brown, 1986, $12.95 (paperback); $22.95 (cloth).		
S784	*Troubled Waters, New Policies for Managing Water in the American West* by Mohamed T. El-Ashry and Diana C. Gibbons, 1986, $7.50.		
S712	*Growing Power: Bioenergy for Development and Industry* by Alan S. Miller, Irving M. Mintzer, and Sara H. Hoagland, 1986, $7.50.		
S725	*Down to Business: Multinational Corporations, the Environment, and Development* by Charles S. Pearson, $7.50		
B723	*The Global Possible: Resources, Development, and the New Century* edited by Robert Repetto, 1986, $13.95 (paperback); $45.00 (cloth).		
B732	*World Enough and Time: Successful Strategies for Resource Management* by Robert Repetto, 1986, $5.95 (paperback); $16.00 (cloth)		
S724	*Getting Tough: Public Policy and the Management of Pesticide Resistance* by Michael Dover and Brian Croft, 1984, $7.50		
S714	*Field Duty: U.S. Farmworkers and Pesticide Safety* by Robert F. Wasserstrom and Richard Wiles, 1985, $7.50		
S716	*A Better Mousetrap: Improving Pest Management for Agriculture* by Michael J. Dover, 1985, $7.50		
S717	*The American West's Acid Rain Test:* by Philip Roth, Charles Blanchard, John Harte, Harvey Michaels, and Mohamed El-Ashry, 1985, $7.50		
S715	*Paying the Price: Pesticide Subsidies in Developing Countries* by Robert Repetto, 1985, $7.50		
S776	*The World Bank and Agricultural Development: An Insider's View* by Montague Yudelman, 1985, $7.50		
S731	*Tropical Forests: A Call for Action,* 1985 by WRI, The World Bank and UNDP, $12.50		
S726	*Helping Developing Countries Help Themselves: Toward a Congressional Agenda for Improved Resource and Environmental Management in the Third World* (a WRI working paper) by Lee M. Talbot, 1985, $10.00		
B721	*World Resources 1986,* $16.95 (paperback); $32.95 (cloth)		
	WRI SUBSCRIPTION $40. ($55 for overseas air mail)		
	TOTAL		

Name _____ (last) _____ (first) _____

Place of Work _____

Street Address _____

City/State _____ Postal Code/Country _____

Please send check or money order (U.S. dollars only) to WRI Publications, P.O. Box 620, Holmes, PA 19043-0620, U.S.A.